The Way of Effortless Leadership:
Ancient Secrets on Cultivating a Culture of Trust, Engagement and Flow

by

K. G. Johnston

Copyright © 2017 by K. G. Johnston

All rights reserved. No part of this book may be reproduced or transmitted in any form by any means, electronic or mechanical, including photocopying, recording or by any information storage and retrieval system without the permission in writing from the author. I have tried to recreate events, locales, and conversations from my memories of them. In order to maintain their anonymity in some instances I have changed the names of individuals and places.

ISBN-13: 978-1-7751768-3-1

Cover and graphics design by Beata Dora Sandor
https://beatasandor.tumblr.com/

Editing and formatting by Wayne Purdin, author of *Pharaoh of the Sun*. wpurdin@gmail.com

The Way of Effortless Leadership

Table of Contents

Testimonials 1

Preface - Business Today 2

Part One: Introduction 4

Chapter 1 – My Story: The Experience That Inspired This Book 5

Chapter 2 – Introduction: It Starts and Ends with You 13

Part Two: Why the Way? 33

Chapter 3 – Why Aren't Things Working? 34

Chapter 4 – What Is the Solution? 37

Chapter 5 – Why Choose Nature's Way? 40

Chapter 6 – We Are All Atmans 43

Chapter 7 – The REAL "Real" World 47

Chapter 8 – Your Life Lens 58

Part Three: The "Model" of the Way 68

Chapter 9 – The Way of Effortless Leadership "Model" 69
   Part 1 – Use Wu Wei 71
   Part 2 - Return to Wu Chi (The Void) 79
   Part 3 - Do Leadership Tai Chi – Flow with the Five Seasons 86
      Winter – Cultivate Self 88
      Spring – Cultivate Culture (Prepare the Soil) 96
      Early Summer – Create and Coach (Plant the Seed and Tend) 107
      Late Summer – Change and Harvest (Reap) 112
      Fall - Consolidate Learning (Plough and Compost) 116

Chapter 10 – Natasha's Story 117

Part Four: Flow 125

Chapter 11 – How to Surf Flow – Meditation in Activity 126

Chapter 12 – Use Yi, Forceless Intention 131

Chapter 13 – Play 133

Chapter 14 – Be "Sung," Mentally and Physically Relaxed 137

Chapter 15 – Be King "Kong" *140*

Chapter 16 – Be "Tzu Jan," Spontaneous and Natural *143*

Chapter 17 – Zhong Din: Keep Moving Stability *145*

Chapter 18 – Be Aware *149*

Chapter 19 – Use Push Hands Principles to Flow with Change and Conflict *154*

Chapter 20 – Work with Paradox *159*

Chapter 21 – Use the Science of Compassion *163*

Chapter 22 – Use Simplicity and Clarity *167*

Chapter 23 – Use Patience *168*

Chapter 24 – Practice Self-Cultivation Mind-Body Exercises *169*

Chapter 25 – Mastery *172*

Part Five: The Way in Business Today **174**

Chapter 26 – Companies That Are Investing in Mind-Body-Spirit Practices *175*

Part Six: Bringing It All Together – Completing the Circle **180**

Chapter 27 – Summary *181*

Note to the Reader **187**

Glossary of Terms and Concepts **188**

Further Reading **190**

End Notes **194**

Acknowledgements

This book is dedicated to you, the human being behind the role of leader. Thank YOU. You could be doing other things with your time, so I'm grateful that I get to share my ideas with you and hope that you find value in what you're about to read.

Tricia, I love you. Following you and making you my wife put into action the forces that led to this book. Your love, support and patience made all the difference. Babe, thanks for believing in me. The bubbly is on me.

Dad, you were my first and best leader. We could always rely on you. Your stillness, wisdom, perception, and way of living still inspire me today. I miss you.

Mum, your steely internal strength to beat cancer thirty-six years ago by changing your thinking, diet, and life is something I admire.

Sis, your irreverent sense of humour, comedic timing, and ability to build trusting long-term relationships amaze me and are reflected in these pages.

My clients over the years, thank you for sharing your experiences and teaching me about effective leadership.

Carol Sachowski. You were a wonderful mentor. You saw me, started me off on this journey, and pushed me through my self-doubt and inertia.

My three favourite bosses over my career: Charlotte, Richard, and Frank. You all demonstrated effortless leadership. You inspired me to do my best work and brought out my natural desire to create and make a difference by seeing me, trusting me, and being interested in my growth. Your humility, relaxed and still energy, compassion, and sense of humour created a peaceful and inspiring culture.

Grand Master (Eddie) Wu Kwong Yu. Sifu (teacher), thank you for making me one of your disciples. Your family's Wu Style tai chi opened my eyes to a new world of internal energy and how to use nature's principle of Wu Wei.

Carol Kerry. It is appropriate that you were born on Valentine's Day, as your compassionate heart is your greatest strength. Watching you grow The East York Gymnastics Club from a small 100 members to the largest in Ontario with over 4,000 members influenced this book.

TESTIMONIALS

"The Way of Effortless Leadership is a journey into one man's personal and professional evolution and offering to the world at large. Displaying vulnerability (strength), passion (intense focus) and humour (love the Yoda and Rush references!), K.G. takes the reader on his quest for an alternate model of leadership that is alive, agile, responsive and respectful on a myriad of levels. Watching him, early on in 2016 physically demonstrate the Wu Wei in a restaurant in downtown Victoria, BC with the aid of his wonderful partner, Tricia, it was all too apparent he was on to something solid - a tangible way of leaders experiencing BEING in Flow when dealing with change or conflict - it stays with you. It's been an honour working with him on this adventure!" — Carol Sachowski, CHRL, CEC, CTC, Coach, Facilitator, Mentor and Consultant

"The tools and insights K.G. shares in his book will elevate leadership to new levels and deliver results. It's required reading for leaders of all levels from supervisor to CEO, looking to play to his or her strength and inspire others to win. What this book delivers, in contrast to many great books on leadership, is embedded in the word 'effortless.' It does not require hard study or memorization. You will feel like you walked into a dark room and someone turned on the light; your reaction will be, "Ahh, now I see!!"I wish this book had been out before my retirement." — C. Katzen, Retired Executive Director of JFSA

"I loved this book. It put me in the right state (calm and meditative) to absorb deep personal insights. It is born from K.G.'s years of exposure to the ways in which the habits, ethics, and energy of leaders profoundly influence their staff. His stories of personal experience ranged from uneasy to inspiring but all were enlightening. The information is thoroughly researched and clearly explained. He presents with grace and humour, a Way, which will organically improve the productivity and atmosphere of your workplace or team. In the 28 years I have known K.G., he has always been a passionate and inspiring motivator." — C. Kerry, Administrator, East York Gymnastics Club, Toronto, ON

The Way of Effortless Leadership

PREFACE - BUSINESS TODAY

> "Come gather round people
> Wherever you roam
> And admit that the waters
> Around you have grown
> And accept it that soon
> You'll be drenched to the bone
> If your time to you
> Is worth savin'
> Then you better start swimmin'
> Or you'll sink like a stone
> For the times they are a changin'."
>
> "Times they are a changing" -Bob Dylan

What are some of the most progressive and successful companies (General Mills, Mckinsey & Company, Google, Apple, Ford, Target, Yahoo, Deutsche Bank, AOL, HBO, Aetna, Samsung, Proctor and Gamble, Intel, Green Mountain Coffee Roasters, Nike etc.) doing? (see Chapter 26 for others and more detailed information)

Why are many of these companies beginning to invest in a new approach to leadership, culture and change?

These organizations have realized that you can increase profits, save money, improve engagement, productivity, creativity, and wellbeing simultaneously. They are beginning to wake up to the many benefits of using ancient wisdom that's thousands of years old but has been largely unknown, forgotten, ignored, or dismissed by us as too simplistic.

The Way is much simpler and more paradoxical than you can imagine. As you read this book, you will come to realize that optimal performance requires the integration of body and mind, feelings and thinking. You will discover that using force is counterproductive and that using awareness, intention, and trust engenders creativity and innovation. Practicing the Way relaxes and revitalizes you, as you see and appreciate the power, wisdom, and beauty of nature's design. You will come to understand that inner change must happen first before you can get external results.

The Way of Effortless Leadership

True leadership is not just about achieving material success but facilitating true prosperity: vitality, growth, well-being, balance, self-expression, connection/love, and realization of potential. A true leader learns how to self-cultivate or self-actualize and help their people do the same.

Following the Way will make your life happier, empower your people, and help you achieve sustainable and effortless business results. My desire is that the Way helps you transform your teams and organizations into places where people feel truly alive, well, empowered, and inspired to give their best to each other so you can thrive together.

When you finish this book, you might say, "It is almost too simple," but I believe that in its simplicity lie its power, beauty, and the reason why it works.

Get ready for a journey. The price of the trip is your ego, hard-held beliefs, exhaustion, frustration, fear, anxiety and desire to control. You don't need to get rid of them, just pack them away in your knapsack. If you love them so much, you can pick them up at the end. So, jump in the raft, hang onto your hat and enjoy the ride.

Keep reading to learn how to go beyond what these companies are doing and reap much greater personal and business benefits.

PART ONE: INTRODUCTION

*"Simplicity, patience, compassion.
These three are your greatest treasures.
Simple in actions and thoughts, you return to the source of being.
Patient with both friends and enemies,
you accord with the way things are.
Compassionate toward yourself,
you reconcile all beings in the world."*

—Lao Tzu, *Tao Te Ching*

"For my ally is the force, and powerful it is."
"Life creates it, makes it grow. Its energy surrounds us and binds us." —Yoda

The Way of Effortless Leadership

Chapter 1 – My Story: The Experience That Inspired This Book

"Nature does not hurry, yet everything is accomplished."
—Lao Tzu

"Shift from being the best in the world to being the best for the world."
— Peter Comrie (Human Capital Specialist)

This chapter is the story of what opened my eyes and led me to see this Way of Effortless Leadership (from now on to be referred to simply as The Way).

My life experiences and those of my clients have led me to the same realization that this Way or "model" is what's been missing in the world of leadership because it mirrors the way the universe works and flows with the real and eternal, doesn't create resistance within people, and enables an agile and fluid response to change. This isn't a fabricated latest trend model, it's wisdom passed down over the millennia by ancient masters that's now supported by current science. I've just combined it with current business terminology. The Way is who you are at core. It allows you to be natural and responsive and to work with human nature in a noncontrived fashion that empowers people.

Throughout the book, I give examples from my life and the lives of others. I don't name people or organizations. I wanted to come from a place of authenticity by sharing my experiences to explain the concepts in this book without harming individuals or organizations. Everyone makes mistakes and is evolving, including me.

I'd been feeling a big change was about to come for a few years but didn't know what it was going to be. Journeys are almost always exciting, rarely predictable, and full of twists and turns, ups and downs, and this is what I was about to experience.

One night, a few years ago, I woke up at three a.m. in the middle of the happiest, most vividly compelling dream of my life. In the dream, I embarked on a journey. My voice from the past whispered to me, "Young man go West." In my dream, I went on a long road trip, moved to the coast, married a beautiful blond-haired woman, and was creating something new and meaningful (not defined). It was a blissful feeling.

So, this middle-aged man with salt and pepper hair sold his condo, threw caution to the wind, and followed the dream. One hot early August morning, I packed up my car in Toronto and hit the road with my rescue dog Mardi and my Mum (who asked if she could come because she loved to travel). I hadn't taken a road trip with my mother since I was a kid. I know, I know…it sounds like a recipe to live the film *National Lampoon's Vacation*. However, the road was long, open, and freeing. The windows were down, and the hot air relaxed us. We took our time and drove through the northern states, took a detour south to check out Wyoming's Yellowstone National Park and then back up through Alberta and across to British Columbia. My mum and I had the chance to just be ourselves without the old roles getting in the way and to connect on a deeper level. We took in the beauty of each place, laughed, listened to music, talked about life, and listened to each other in a way that we hadn't done before. When we drove through the town of Hope towards the coast, I felt like I was coming home. My mum flew back to Toronto when we arrived in Vancouver but still recounts this trip as one of her favourite. It was a great trip; we simply got to BE with each other. The concept of simply BEING with another person is important in this Way.

Vancouver's fresh ocean air energized me and cleared my head. I walked everywhere and loved being surrounded by the natural beauty of the mountains and the ocean. I found a job and lucked out with an excellent boss, Charlotte, who inspired me. In my spare time, I decided to do as the British Columbians do; I took up hiking, meditation, yoga, and guitar.

A year later, I met a woman who captured my heart who resembled the woman in my dream. Tricia lived across the Strait of Georgia on the outskirts of Nanaimo, and within a year, I proposed to her. I decided to leave my job to follow love since Tricia had more ties on the Island. It wasn't an easy decision because Charlotte asked me if I would stay and offered me the position of Director of Employment Services. Life was wonderful and I felt on top of the world.

Tricia lived in a rural area. The house was on acreage and secluded. I felt that I had wandered into the forest and was feeling lost. The property overlooked a small lake and a valley that's shared with eagles, dragonflies, rabbits, deer, quail, trees, blackberries, flowers,

The Way of Effortless Leadership

and the occasional bear. I had always loved visiting nature but found living in it day to day was a huge adjustment for a city boy. The isolation from all of the city's busyness made me feel like a hermit monk.

I began realizing just how much my ego and identity were tied to my work. I found myself in a strange place with very little industry and no networking contacts. Despite lots of effort and DOING, I wasn't HAVING the results I wanted. Since there was a lack of options, I chose a couple of employers who weren't a good fit for me. This was the winter of my vocational discontent.

In between searching for work, I worked on our house and around our property. I communed with nature, practiced yoga, meditation, and tai chi during breaks and even tried my hand at organic vegetable gardening. Being away from the hectic rush of the business world of big egos, the quiet sanity of nature's simplicity began changing me and modelling what I needed to learn. It was as if nature were opening me up to something much larger than my personal sense of self and goals. I started seeing connections in everything that I was learning and surrounded with. I came face-to-face with my own ego, competitiveness, arrogance, impatience, and desire to control events.

I began to experience why great Eastern thinkers used nature and this life force as their inspiration and model of leadership, well-being/health, and growth.

> *"As you start to walk out on the way, the way appears."* —Rumi

Little by little, I began to see everything differently. I became more and more aware of the beauty, effectiveness, effortlessness, and subtlety of nature's system of creation and growth. Small changes in one part of the ecosystem affected the whole system. Stillness and movement were perfectly balanced. There was a feeling of timelessness all around me. This intelligent and powerful life force energy flowed effortlessly amongst all things. Every life form was like a wave of existence. Nature was aware, energetic, vibrant, sensual, playful, and interdependent. The aliveness, colour, and individual expression of everything jumped out at me. I was amazed at how fast plants and trees would push up through our asphalt driveway and grow back after I cut them, even ones we thought were dead. This life force inspired, amazed, and sometimes frustrated me, as there was no way to hold it back. Balance, diversity, and uniqueness were everywhere. Watching the humming birds and the bees pollinating flowers highlighted their interdependence. Instead of seeing an undifferentiated monolithic forest, I saw—I really saw— each of the trees as unique beings with individual markings and personalities. Plants and animals were keenly aware and responsive to subtle energy shifts in the environment. There were long dormant periods followed by insane, nonstop growth, followed by another period of quiet dormancy, and this cycle repeated itself. Gardeners and farmers who may be reading this are probably saying, "Really! That's nothing new," but for me **the direct experience of nature's perfect efficiency** was an eye-opening breakthrough.

It was at this low period of not being able to see my career forest for the trees that I decided to get a mentor and coach. Carol Sachowski took the time and energy to uncover my passion. Carol's belief in me at this difficult time in my life is something for which I'm forever grateful. She encouraged me to develop my own leadership model, which became this book. In the process, I discovered that I loved to write and that I wanted to learn more about this craft, pursue it, and see where it would lead me.

I read voraciously, took courses, and watched TED Talk and YouTube videos on a wide variety of business and personal topics. My knowledge of meditation, tai chi chuan, and yogic/vedic philosophy and their understanding of the universe began to make sense at a much deeper level. Many businesses are discovering the benefits of teaching their people these ancient mind-body disciplines because they improve productivity, decrease stress, and save them money. However, most don't understand that these ancient systems were designed to help people connect to nature's original underlying design and flow. I had always wanted to make a difference to the quality of leadership because leaders influence all aspects of our lives and what we see as possible. I saw an opportunity to show leaders and wannabe leaders how they could use this ancient wisdom in business to achieve high employee engagement and buy-in for change.

My education and work in human resources, change management, coaching, talent management and career counselling has given me insight into what people want and need in their lives. My time as a consultant provided me with insights most people don't get to experience. I had the opportunity to witness many different organizations with very different cultures and leadership styles and learn what both empowered and disempowered individuals, teams, and cultures. Leaders create the culture by their way of being and

The Way of Effortless Leadership

modelling. Walking into an organization, I would sense what was happening by watching faces and body language and listening to the sounds in the office. Corporate culture is just like the culture of a country or any group of people. It's the shared beliefs, assumptions, norms of the people about what's important and encouraged and what's discouraged. Culture has a profound effect on people's well-being, behaviour, and performance. It can bring out the best or the worst in individuals. Corporate culture is like invisible air that always surrounds us and impacts talent retention, team spirit, and communication. The air can be like fresh oxygen that invigorates, or toxic, choking us and making us run for the exit.

Few organizations did things well during times of change because the leaders lost track of how they were BEING with their people and put too much focus on task oriented DOING and HAVING. Many were fearful that their people would find out that they really didn't have the answers and had to feign strength and confidence.

Despite all the intense DOING, most change didn't work very well and was often damaging to both those who stayed and left the organization. They gave off a distant, cool, and hardened "Big Boss" air of self-importance, looking busy and "impressive" and DOING a lot but not being efficient and effective. They approached their work with an **"It's not personal, it's just business"** mentality. *However, I can tell you with certainty that people experience change very personally!* Most leaders didn't know their people well and were usually wrong in how they thought each of their people would react to change. Many leaders appeared to have checked their humanity at the door in the name of being "professional" and acted in ways that didn't honour their better nature. Most people were fearful and distrustful of leaders, especially in times of great change. Some leaders confided in me that they felt the system forced them to behave in a way in which they didn't believe and which was unnatural to them.

> **"When people lose their fear of power**
> **Then great power has indeed arrived"**
> —Lao Tzu, *Tao Te Ching* (72)

In addition, I had the privilege of career and life coaching hundreds of people and facilitating groups of diverse individuals. I learnt that most people have an insatiable desire to grow, change, self-express, create, and contribute, yet employee engagement is very low. So,

WHAT is happening? Why can't more leaders harness the natural drive within all of us?

The clients I coached shared their stories with me and taught me what leaders did that either demotivated or engaged them. Almost every client said that ranked/rated structured performance appraisals didn't inspire them to improve their performance. In fact, they demotivated them. They felt that most leaders not only didn't inspire them but they also suppressed their natural drive to create, contribute, and serve because they didn't feel seen, heard, or appreciated and part of the building process. The small percentage of leaders who did things well, had a different energy, character, focus, and mantra. They had a very different vibe, and they put the focus on how they were BEING with their people.

My clients taught me that all those things (missions, visions, values, strategies, projects, products, programs, and initiatives) of which leaders were so proud only engaged them if they felt that leaders sincerely cared about them as individuals and were making a difference to the world, not just making money. Plaques on walls, corporate speak, and words on websites, if not authentic and lived by leaders, made things worse. When people felt that leaders were unnatural and rehearsed, using the latest technique or model on them, they felt manipulated, disempowered, and even more disengaged.

The quality and consistency of leadership and the cultural climate was what my clients were interested in. As business author Peter Drucker said, "Culture eats strategy for breakfast." But what exactly is culture and where do you really need to begin to truly shift it to empower people?

My clients described culture as being primarily the quality and consistency of the leaders' characters and BEING. They weren't impressed by a powerful and confident image, brilliance, or what leaders developed. What they wanted was a safe, harmonious, appreciative, and peaceful environment in which they could be self-expressive, grow, collaborate, and be trusted to do their best work. My clients spoke about how they could feel a manager's intentions towards them, and this correlated directly to their level of engagement, creativity, and performance. It was the "vibes" that leaders gave off individually and as a leadership team and how these vibrations and expectations either demotivated or motivated them. The leaders' inner being and self-awareness was what created the culture as they modelled the way to be. Top leaders were frequently

The Way of Effortless Leadership

described as being in good physical/mental shape, having an inner sense of peace, grounded, centered, aware, calm, passionate, content, patient, humble, warm, and compassionate with a good sense of humour and a relaxed perspective that could be felt. Edgy, self-impressed, distant, secretive, cold, fixated, unaware, self-promoting, uncaring, and lacking sincere empathy characterized the most disliked and distrusted leaders. The worst leaders viewed people as resources to get the job done, whereas the best leaders didn't have a utilitarian view of their people but truly saw their value and uniqueness. People told me that culture was all about what was encouraged and discouraged and **how leaders viewed them and how they made them feel about themselves and their potential.**

Athena McKenzie, in an article in *Douglas Magazine*'s June/July 2016 edition titled "Does Intimacy Belong in Your Business?" interviewed Jordan Bower "strategic storyteller" who believes we live in the "age of loneliness." Jordan referred to a Google workplace study that determined that five factors distinguish successful teams. The most important factor by far was "psychological safety." Bower said, "Psychological safety in my language is akin to intimacy." Bower asks leaders to "recognize that people process their world through emotions, and to incorporate qualities of human relationships such as trust, honesty, and vulnerability in their messaging."

To give you a taste of where we're going, I'd like to share a story of one company that stood out head and shoulders above the rest. The company was restructuring and undergoing change and staff reductions. The first day I walked in as a consultant to lead a workshop, I was taken aback. Those who were to be let go at the end of a notice period were smiling, laughing, and joking around with each other. You could feel the love! The sound in the office was more like that of a happy and playful schoolyard, yet everyone was very attentive and focused. When their managers came into the room, the positive vibes got even stronger and more playful. I got curious and asked the crowd why they felt so positive at an obviously difficult time for them. They said the leaders were humble and had developed this incredible spirit of oneness and purpose, and they felt they had created something great together. Teams shared information, ideas, and resources. The people said their leaders were genuine and consistently demonstrated that they cared about them, their personal development, and their careers. The leaders had shown each of them respect and treated them like family. Some of the leaders had already found jobs in other companies for their people and the rest were actively searching for them. There was a spirit of

"All for one and one for all." They were encouraged to take risks, to innovate, and to develop themselves. The leaders had communicated early and openly about the state of business and the things that drove the business, so there was no surprise when word came down about the change. The group said that they were proud of their legacy and wanted to leave it in better shape than when they came, and they wanted to return when times got better. This experience inspired me. The leaders put their attention into developing a culture that made people feel good about themselves and their contribution, and, in turn, the leaders earned their trust, energy, loyalty, engagement, creativity, and love like I've never seen before. This was effortless leadership in action.

This Way of Effortless Leadership rehumanizes leadership and encourages you to take off your armour and develop what mystic Sadhguru calls "an inclusive consciousness." It will teach you how to change your vibes. It will ask you to relax any rigid ideas you have about yourself and other people. It offers you a simple way to become a leader who inspires and brings out the best in you and your people while achieving effortless results. It is about seeing yourself as the seed from which everyone and everything will grow. It is about turning inward to become outwardly effective.

Chapter 2 – Introduction: It Starts and Ends with You

New Paradigm: Reunite with Nature's Flow and Come Back into Balance

"If there is no transformation inside of us, all the structural change in the world will have no impact on our institutions." –Peter Block
(organizational consultant)

The quote by Peter Block above speaks to the heart of this book. So, before getting into this chapter, I invite you to turn to Chapter 8, Your Life Lens, and complete the self-awareness exercises. Doing so, will allow you to begin this journey by deepening your understanding of how you see and experience the world. This way or "model" starts and ends with you and how you see people, the world, and their relationship.

Here are a few questions to get you thinking before we get started. Be brutally honest with yourself. No one is looking.

> **Do you REALLY believe you understand and you have the answers in this chaotic ever-changing world?** If not, how do you deal with your own fear and uncertainty about constant change at work? Do you pretend that you know and exert more control and command? Or, are you honest and transparent and enlist your people to try to improvise to deal with it.
>
> **Why should your people follow YOU?**
>
> **Would your people follow you if you weren't paying them or paying them less?** Do they share your vision or do they grudgingly put in their time working for you because you wield power over their livelihood, career, reputation, and financial security?
>
> **When have you felt most alive, engaged, connected and in touch with something profound and real?** At work? Probably not. Most of your people don't have that experience at work either.

How well do you really see, know, and appreciate each of your people? Or, do you see them as replaceable resources or units of production to get tasks accomplished?

Have you ever held your tongue and maintained organizational silence on an issue that went against what you knew was right, your core values, or basic humanity at work?

Has your company ever created something or done something that's harmful to nature, animals, or people? How did you react?

Do you often feel that information doesn't flow up to you?

Have you ever done something or treated someone in a way you knew wasn't right out of self-interest or because you felt the system demanded it?

Congratulations, you're the boss. You're the boss, my condolences. You're one of the few who have "made it." You have positional power. You're making good money. Your ego is massaged. You can implement your ideas. You have autonomy. You have influence. People are required to listen to you.

Leadership is or should be about accomplishing meaningful goals that improve human experience through the ideas and energy of others. In my experience, you have only two ways to approach this challenge.

1. You can distrust your people, manage, force, control, coerce, or bribe them.

or

2. You can trust your people, share your desires for a better world or model, and get them excited about building it together, give them the climate and resources they need and get out of their way.

Someone's view of how the world operates and who people are in the greater scheme of things is key. The first approach comes from a place of superiority/inferiority, separation, and fear. The latter comes from a place of equality, unity, and love. The challenge is to discover

The Way of Effortless Leadership

what people want and need to bring out their natural drive to learn, create, change, perform, and achieve. It's much simpler than you thought. This way IS NOT about using the carrot or the stick to engage your people.

> *"Punishment and Reward proceed from basically the same psychological mode; one that conceives of motivation as nothing more than manipulation of behaviour." Alfie Kohn*

If you're like most leaders, you've discovered that your positional power is a two-edged sword that often cuts deep and it isn't as rewarding as you had hoped.

Have you experienced any of the following?

- Worried that people will discover that you don't have the answers.
- A cluttered mind.
- Work has lost its fun.
- You're not getting buy-in for your initiatives.
- You aren't trusted.
- You can't be spontaneous.
- Alone, disconnected, and out of touch from others.
- What you do fails to motivate and empower your people.
- Split, having to separate your work and home selves.
- Unappreciated.
- Exhausted from pushing your people to produce and trying to force change.
- Your organization or team vibrates with discord and disharmony.
- Cold wars between departments, where information fails to flow.
- Your people are cynical and resigned.
- Your people lack energy and self-expression.
- What you know and do doesn't seem to empower people.
- You're weighted down by a crushing amount of complexity in your work.
- You're leery of giving trust and delegating.
- You feel cynical and resigned to just making a living and not a difference.
- Your people, team, and business are not performing to their potential.
- You don't sleep well at night.

- Your physical or psychological issues are exacerbated by stress at work.
- You don't have breathing space, thinking space, or peace of mind.

WHAT IS THE OPPORTUNITY?

Well, what if you could experience some or all of the following?
- Relax more, let go, do less, trust more, and achieve more.
- Bring out the natural drive and creativity in your people.
- Be yourself.
- Be spontaneous.
- Have more energy.
- Make an indelible positive shift in your company culture.
- Achieve higher attraction, engagement, creativity, productivity, and retention.
- Help your organization be an employer of choice.
- Enjoy an irrepressible energy and collaboration at work.
- Deal better with stress and have more fun at work.
- Have more work/life balance.
- Have much lower levels of company absenteeism, sickness, and disability claims.
- Be healthier and happier.
- Be more at peace with yourself and those around you.
- Be the kind of boss others remember fondly as that pivotal person in their personal and professional lives who helped them learn, grow, self-actualize, and evolve.
- Feel a greater sense of connection to others.
- Be the drop that ripples out and transforms society's work culture.

If what you had to do was counterintuitive and paradoxical and required you to

1. focus less on DOING and achieving/HAVING results,
2. focus on what you have direct control over, your internal experience or way of BEING (thinking, feeling, and perceiving), and this would
3. transform you, your people, your culture, and, ultimately, your results,

would you do it?

The Way of Effortless Leadership

"The way to do is to be." —Lao Tzu

You've been entrusted with the mantle of power. You impact people's personal and professional lives to a profound degree. Don't underestimate the weight your vibrations, words, tone of voice, expressions, behaviour, ideas, and way of being/presence have on people. Years later, people will remember how you made them feel about themselves, how they grew, and what they created together.

Ask yourself. Am I willing to:

- See the world with clear eyes?
- See myself anew?
- Become aware of my energy and shift it?
- See my people differently?
- Relax my ego?
- Empty my cup and let go of all I think I know?
- Be real, open, and transparent?
- Be vulnerable?
- Put my people first and get out of their way?

If yes, you're halfway there. If not, you might not be ready for this Way just yet.

"You must unlearn what you have learned." —Yoda

OLD MECHANISTIC PARADIGM OF SEPARATION AND UNSUSTAINABILITY

I wrote this book because, from my experience as a consultant and coach, I noticed that business, as a system, is dysfunctional and doesn't empower leaders, their people, or the planet. The state of the world and our organizations are dependent on the quality of the internal states of our leaders. This is true not only in business but also in government, education, nonprofits, and religious organizations.

So, what's happening in our world and organizations today? What are the unspoken underlying paradigm, assumptions, and principles that create the game we play?

In Eric Michael Johnson's article, "Survival of the...Nicest? Check Out the Other Theory of Evolution," he wrote,

> A century ago, the industrialists like Andrew Carnegie believed that Darwin's theories justified an economy of vicious competition and inequality. They left us with an ideological legacy that says corporate economy, in which wealth concentrates in the hands of a few, produces the best for humanity. This was always a distortion of Darwin's ideas. His 1871 book *The Descent of Man* argued that the human species had succeeded because of traits like sharing and compassion.

The system has taken on a life of its own and operates on automatic, and our choices are determined by it. Our system isn't modelled on the natural world. It's a human creation that's based on fear, scarcity, greed, competition, selfishness, and ego and encourages and celebrates our worst qualities as we attempt to gain control and attain security. Everything is complex, we're rushed, and we've become hardened. It doesn't support life, well-being, or self-actualization. Leaders have few truly effective and inspirational models to follow. Integrity seems to have been replaced by protection of self-interest. Leaders have tremendous pressure to be the saviors who swoop in and introduce brilliant initiatives that transform organizations. Many well-meaning leaders feel they must change who they are to survive and succeed in the world of business. This makes them feel misunderstood, isolated, and unappreciated. Workers often feel like cogs in a wheel, to be used and then replaced at the whim of management. The planet is being used in an unsustainable way. This creates a system that has taken on a life of its own and devalues all of us.

The following will be controversial to many of you and was to me, but my own competitive nature was effectively challenged after reading the award-winning book, *No Contest*. Author Alfie Kohn says that our societal system (our education, our recreation, our relationships, our work, etc.), which is built on the assumption that everything is a competition and that "my success requires your failure," isn't an inevitable part of human nature. He makes a strong case that competition doesn't build character but, instead, ruins individuals' self-esteem and relationships. Games and activities that encourage mastery don't require competition. **Kohn makes a compelling point that competition creates scarcity where there was none.**

The Way of Effortless Leadership

The founder of Organizational Development, Richard Beckhard, said that one goal of a healthy organization is to develop "open communication, mutual trust, confidence between all levels." He said that teams are the building blocks of an organization; so, to achieve a healthy organizational state, one must "reduce competition and increase collaboration."

The 2008 Financial Crisis revealed cracks in our system that seemed as big as The San Andreas Fault. I believe it was a small shock wave and a warning of a large systemic quake to come.

Director Michael Moore claims in his film *Capitalism – A Love Story* that Corporations are treated in Law as persons. A corporation isn't a living being that's part of the natural world, and providing it the same rights that we enjoy has created the problem. For more information on this topic, see the Recommended Reading section's Articles on Corporate Personhood. In addition, Moore makes the point that it's a bit ironic that we cherish our democratic ideals, yet organizations are often autocratic (except for employee owned ones). We've created an operating system that works on automatic that puts profit and expansion above all else. In turn, corporations hire and promote people who hold these values.

The legal system and the stock market are both atomistic and don't take into consideration unintended consequences. They're based on greed and fear and have lost an ethical grounding. The rules of the legal system and the financial system are so complex that only a select few really understand them, and this creates inequality.

Corporations make record profits and eliminate jobs to show more profit.

Advertising creates a never-ending need within us for things we don't need. We, as consumers, put pressure on companies to create cheaper goods, setting up a system that focuses on continually reducing the cost of production without concern for the livelihood and security of the people making the things.

Many individuals are promoted to leadership positions because of their technical skills and not their character, ethics, and soft people skills, and they do more harm than good. They seek leadership for self-interest and self-enrichment. In a 2015 Fortune.com article "Top CEOs Make More Than 300 Times the Average Worker," Paul

Hodgson states "In between 1978 and 2014, inflation-adjusted CEO pay increased by almost 1,000%" and "up by 54.3% since the recovery began in 2009. Meanwhile most other workers have faced stagnant wages." It is well known that when the divide between the rich and poor becomes extreme, revolution happens and systems change.

Burnout and mental health issues are the major challenges for both individuals and organizations. A January 1, 2017 Fortune.com article "New French Law Bars Work Email After Hours" says, "A new French law established workers 'right to disconnect' goes into effect today." People are working longer hours and are continuously leashed to the office by email on their downtime, creating burnout. The article points out "a group of Stanford business professors have estimated that workplace stress added between $125 and $190 billion dollars a year to America's healthcare costs."

Where are we heading?

Do you remember the Ridley Scott film *Bladerunner,* in which corporations rule and have ruined the natural world and people's relationships with each other? Humans' lives are controlled by the system. The humans display a lack of humanity and live in a dark, dirty, paranoid, and impersonal world. The people live unconsciously, playing out the game, and bioengineered replicants are more human than the people, displaying kindness and compassion to each other, making Deckhard (Harrison Ford's character) question his own humanity, as the replicants strive to escape being retired or killed by him and other bladerunners (human bounty hunters) and extend their lives. At the end of the film, one of the main characters, Roy saves Deckhard from falling to his death and then says, "All those moments lost in time, like tears in the rain. Time to die." The last scene in the original release shows Deckhard and Rachael (replicant) flying into a green and blue nature setting. Science fiction? Or, foreshadowing of things to come?

We know in our gut that the system doesn't work but we don't believe we have the power to start fixing it. Our options are controlled by the system that operates unconsciously and automatically. The game often brings out the worst in us but the good news is you can chip away at the game by leading and modelling a better way for your people.

The Way of Effortless Leadership

"Most 'necessary evils' are far more evil than necessary."—Sir Richard Branson

The earth has unlimited resources and is there for us to exploit. Recycling won't work, as people won't spend time separating their garbage. The world is flat. Slavery is good for business. Witches are evil and should be burned at the stake. Women are men's property. Gays are defective and must be killed, punished, or jailed. The disabled have little to offer. Communism and the Cold War will never end. Apartheid will always exist.

"And the sign said long-haired freaky people need not apply." – "Signs" – Song by the Canadian band, Five Man Electrical Band

Shaking your head? This shows our evolution and our ability to see, think, and feel differently, to change our paradigms, assumptions, prejudices, and beliefs. People who bring new ways of seeing have enabled us to view our relationship to reality and each other more accurately and compassionately.

Anytime that a new paradigm is proposed, the establishment feels threatened by it and there's strong opposition to it before it's proven and eventually adopted.

Before the 1500s, the predominant view was that our world was the center of the universe and that everything revolved around us. Gailileo Gallilei challenged the existing paradigm in his book *The Dialogue Concerning the Two Chief World Systems,* but was arrested and forced to recant his beliefs because it was contrary to the Catholic Church's worldview. We know now that old belief is false and that we're just a tiny speck of stardust in a never-ending universe.

We used to think that the universe worked in a Newtonian mechanical way (think balls on a pool table colliding with each other in an impersonal way) but over the last hundred years, the new science has proven that:

Everything in the universe is relational and does not, at its deepest level, operate mechanically and separately but energetically, systemically, and holistically.

Unfortunately, the way we see and interact with the world and each other hasn't caught up with the science. We still perceive ourselves as separate entities who collide with each other from time to time.

So, being a leader, you have a choice. You can either be an:

- Old paradigm (Newtonian) mechanical leader and see yourself as a pool player with a cue, whacking balls (your people) **forcing them to move**.

OR a

- New paradigm (Quantum/Super String/Neuroscience) living systems leader and view yourself as a musician who plays a catchy tune that **naturally moves your people**.

You will learn more about the science in Chapter 7, The REAL "Real" World.

The 2016 Paris Agreement on climate change shows world leadership is increasingly waking up to the ecological, climate and human ramifications of separating ourselves from nature and each other, fixating on goals, being rigid in our thinking, not seeing holistically and treating resources as inexhaustible. We've begun to experience extreme destructive weather, global warming, air pollution, rising sea levels, deforestation, damage to animal habitats, loss of quality soil/minerals due to land overuse, food shortages (increased prices), health issues, and the ongoing global financial crisis. The experts predict that climate change will increase social upheaval and lead to war. The divide between rich and poor is getting wider. Our myopic unnatural and unsustainable concept of growth and drive for "progress" and "wealth" has paradoxically led us into a potentially catastrophic future.

"The Industrial Age is not sustainable in ecological terms, and it's not sustainable in human terms." —Peter Senge

I challenge the continued belief that business is the "real world" and that it operates outside of the natural world, free from consequence. We, as a species, are narcissistic and have operated from a belief that we are superior and separate from all else. We've treated animals as automatons without consciousness and feelings and separated them

The Way of Effortless Leadership

from the land to use them as products for our convenience. We've polluted our oceans. We've clear-cut old forests that provide us with oxygen. We've messed with nature's balance in our food, commercializing and processing the minerals and nutrients out of it. We've created GMOs, hybrid wheat to get higher yields to make more profit. This tampering with nature's bounty has been damaging to our heath by unintentionally creating huge increases in allergies and inflammatory and autoimmune diseases.

I suggest that we as leaders have lost our connection to the natural world and to each other. We've created an unhealthy business climate that's ineffective, inefficient, and wasteful because it works against our human nature and Mother Nature. We've gotten off a proven natural path and made simple things complicated to boost our ego, look "impressive," and "distinguish" ourselves from nature, animals, and each other. In the process of trying to outsmart nature, we've unintentionally created pollution, dis-ease, disharmony, stress, and illness and lack of engagement/satisfaction, innovation, and productivity in our organizations. Our strong desire to compete is a short-term, ego-driven, dualistic, win-lose mentality that's completely contrary to nature. Nature is about survival and mutual long-term growth.

***"Our Western science ever since the 17th century has been obsessed with the notion of control, of man dominating nature. This obsession has led to disaster." *– **Fritjof Capra (Physicist, Systems Theorist)**

The belief that business is the "real world" is strange and false. It's humans trying to impose themselves on the natural order of things. We've lost our natural instincts and have put too much faith in mechanical systems. We've been blind to nature's intelligence, thinking it was too simple or primitive, yet nature has refined, evolved, and continued to perfect its systems over billions of years, starting from single-celled life in water, well before we inhabited our shared world.

In times where everyone worked on the land, we were at one with it. We felt our reliance and integration with it. We understood and flowed with natural cyclical rhythms. Our mind and body worked as one whole. Work lost its connection to the natural world in the early 1800s. The industrial revolution created a new paradigm in the way we view people and work. In the new system, work was separated from the rest of our life, we moved away from extended families to get jobs. People and nature were now seen and treated as tools, resources, and production units. They weren't valued for their own sake. We didn't choose this system but, rather, were born into it. Now, in our modern society, we sit all day and use our intellect. We've lost the connection between our body and mind and have disregarded the importance of emotion, feeling, and spirit. Nature is holistic and our actions have created unintended consequences.

I'm not suggesting we go back to living off the land but that we treat nature with reverence and respect, feel our connection to her, and use her as a model and mentor and get out of her way. In doing so, we'll honour our own humanity and individuality.

Our world has evolved and there's been a lot of social progress in terms of material gains and improvements in human rights, health, democracy, and appreciation of diversity; but if you could ask the other living beings on our planet, most wouldn't say life has improved. New technology (video, the Internet and social media) has expanded our consciousness by allowing us to share ideas and information instantly, and has impacted our view of leadership. The old military command and control model of leadership doesn't work to inspire. In the past, we blindly trusted our leaders and institutions, but that's largely gone the way of the dinosaur. We're turning away from institutions and leaders that have used force and control to suppress the human spirit. People are seeking leaders who will facilitate their self-realization. People are seeking truth beyond labels and "isms." Turf wars are fought because of group identification and contrasting the good "us" against bad "them." Being human is a holistic experience that we share with all others and the planet itself. When we separate ourselves from others by identifying with groups or labels, we limit our experience, understanding, and ability to perceive our deeper selves. People are seeking leaders who are worthy of them and who will share power with them to create a better world. I believe that instead of continually challenging others' ideas, our freedom will come from challenging our own.

We're not reaching our potential because we haven't kept up with the current understanding of the **interdependency of nature/universe and human nature**. We've stopped seeing our world, others, and ourselves accurately and for the sentient beings that we are.

When we feel separate and alone, it makes us feel alienated, insecure, and want to hoard money and possessions to gain a temporary feeling of security and protection in a perceived "dog-eat-dog" world.

The Way of Effortless Leadership

Paradoxically, in our attempt to maintain control, we don't feel that we're in control, that things are okay, and that we can relax. This creates an institutionalized lack of empathy and a psychopathology. Possessions, money, and recognition are fine, but to achieve a better quality of life, our myopic focus on accumulating is contrary to nature's abundant way, and is disempowering, disconnecting and diseasing our people.

NEW QUANTUM/STRING THEORY LIVING SYSTEM PARADIGM OF UNITY AND SUSTAINABILITY

This Way is a new paradigm that's as old as time. My aim is to take lessons from new science and ancient wisdom and make this an easy read and simple to use so that it doesn't become just another book on your shelf. My hope is that it resonates with you at a deep level and that you use it to bring out the best in you and your people.

"Before the beginning of great brilliance, there must be chaos. Before a brilliant person begins something great, they must look foolish in the crowd." – I Ching

LOOK TO NATURE

"Look deep into nature, and then you will understand everything better." —Albert Einstein

Where do you feel your best? Where do you feel most alive? Where do you feel most grounded, connected, and well? If you're like most people, a beautiful nature scene popped into your head. Think about how your body, mind, and spirit change when you walk barefoot on the grass or sand and take in the sights, sounds, and scents of nature. Your breathing changes, your awareness expands, stress dissolves, your face relaxes, you feel more, and you think more clearly. Nature reconnects you to what's alive, basic, and real.

You're going to reconnect with nature, let go of unhelpful mental models, beliefs, and conditioning and forego the reliance on force and strategy. Instead, you'll develop your energy, character, and awareness and allow yourself to be natural and spontaneous.

This Way or "Model" has three simple parts:
1. Use her one simple principle.
2. Tap nature's force and follow her way.
3. Follow her transformational growth cycle.

We're sentient human BEINGS yet we act like human DOINGS and mere consumers. We operate on and emit energy and are surrounded by electromagnetic fields. Have you ever felt an immediate comfort and sense of trust (or discomfort and distrust) in someone you just met before anything was done or said to warrant your assessment? Recently, neuroscientists have discovered that our vagus nerve is a feedback loop from our gut to our brain. Our immediate gut instincts like fear are sent to the brain just as our thoughts are sent back down to the gut and organs via this nerve. It is a self-organizing system and is part of the mind-body connection that works on vibrational signals. This book will help you learn to cultivate your character and vibrational energy so the signals you give off to your people will elicit relaxation and trust so they can feel better, stop being self-protective/concerned, become more aware, think more clearly, and put their attention on your shared goals and work at hand.

How you're being and acting either frees up or constrains your people.

"When you are content to be simply yourself and don't compare or compete, everyone will respect you." —Lao Tzu, *Tao Te Ching*

This Way isn't some new-fangled business model. **It's the opposite of a set of preprogrammed techniques or models.** Techniques are artificial and only work in certain contexts. Nature's way is simple; effortless; doesn't require hard thought or memorization; allows for the unexpected and unpredictable; and enables you to react quickly, naturally, and spontaneously regardless of circumstance. Leading this way is a freeing and creative experience.

This Way requires expanded awareness, inclusiveness, honesty, sincerity, vulnerability, trust, and clear positive intent. If you come with the intention to use this Way as a technique to control or outsmart your people, it won't work; you'll lose their trust, and it will backfire. **It's about getting present with nature, yourself, and your people.** It's a natural growth process that operates on universal principles (that often seem paradoxical), which enable flexible responsive movement to any change.

The Way of Effortless Leadership

In *The Sustainable Advantage,* Percy Willard wrote,

> Conventional business wisdom is wrong. To wake us up, we need new paradigms or models of reality. To feel responsibility for social conditions and the environment, corporations' "mental model" of the economy's relationship with society and the environment needs to be almost reversed. The traditional business view places the environment and society as separate entities, outside economic considerations and miniscule in relative importance. Conventional business intuition mistakenly sees priorities in economic, environmental, and social policy as competing. A more accurate frame of reference would reverse this perspective and acknowledge that the global economy is a small sector within global society, which, in turn, is within the global environment that's necessary for life as we know it.

Following this Way will create healthy sustainable growth that doesn't harm and, instead, heals and nurtures. It's the way of life. It's the way of water. We're 70% water. All life came from water and requires water to live. Pure water is perfectly balanced with a PH level of 7. This Way is about increasing conscious awareness and achieving a **natural state of flow that nourishes** everything and everyone.

> *"Water is fluid, soft, and yielding. But water will wear away rock, which is rigid and cannot yield. As a rule, whatever is fluid, soft, and yielding will overcome whatever is rigid and hard. This is another paradox: what is soft is strong."* —Lao Tzu

You are the high-quality seed in this model that will allow you, your people, teams, and organization to grow and be well. It requires that you lose the old fear-based scarcity mindset and open to the idea that there's more than enough to go around and to adopt a paradigm based on abundance. Instead of using reductionist atomistic thinking, you'll be asked to use holistic living systems thinking.

INSPIRATIONS

Indigenous people around the world have always known that nature is our best mentor and ally and that we have a responsibility to take care of her. They believe that we don't own anything but rather borrow it from nature for a short time. I believe that if we show her respect and follow her lead, we'll experience greater joy, happiness, and bliss; achieve greater results with less effort; and gain the respect and loyalty of our people and our customers with ease.

This Way is inspired primarily by Lao Tzu's explanation of the *I Ching (Book of Changes)* in his book the *Tao Te Ching* (Taoism) and application of its principles in tai chi chuan, traditional Chinese medicine, and qigong. The *I Ching (Book of Changes)* was the original and, in my opinion, best change management book of all time.

The *Tao Te Ching* is one of the most published books of all time. **Tao means the "Way."** All experienced martial artists seek to use it. It teaches us **how nature/the universe works**. It shows us a way we can live in harmony with nature by tapping its one source of intelligence, using one key principle, **"Wu Wei"** (Effortless or Forceless Action) and being **"De"** (living or flowing in accordance with the Tao or nature's way). Following the Way or the Tao means getting out of nature's way, flowing with its design, and learning to find stillness in movement and movement in stillness. It's all about health, awareness, and growth.

This Way provides leaders a way to trust and reconnect to their own internal intelligence, work in harmony with nature and human nature, and have their work be elegantly efficient without wasting energy, polluting or creating unintended problems. This model, from here on, will be referred to simply as "the Way."

The Way also borrows concepts from and is in harmony with Buddhism, yogic, and indigenous beliefs, as they all have similar paradigms or worldviews that point us in the same direction.

In Christina Brown's book *The Book of Yoga*, she explains:

> The word *yoga* originates from the Sanskrit *yuj*. Yuj may be translated as to 'center one's thoughts,' 'to concentrate oneself,' or 'to meditate deeply.' All of these things involve the slowing of the movements of the mind. From *yuj* also come 'unite,' 'join,' and 'connect,' which imply a reintegration, a bringing back into balance.

You'll stop the incessant rushing and nonstop doing and regain peace of mind, reintegrating parts of yourself, and come back into balance.

The Way of Effortless Leadership

This enables you to lead from a centered, still, and elegantly effective place.

You'll be introduced to Eastern, Taoist, and Hindu concepts and terms. Turn to the Glossary at the back of the book. The first concept is **qi or chi or "breath of life" or "energy flow."** In yoga, it's called prana. In *Star Wars*, qi is called "the force." It's the universal intelligent life-force energy that animates and connects everything. Feeling it and learning how to let it flow freely is important in this way. When felt, it gives us broader perspective, insight, and internal power.

"May the force be with you" —Yoda

Some inspired individuals like Janine Benyus have seen the future by looking to nature. Janine Benyus is a biologist who co-founded The Biomimicry Institute. She acts as a consultant to large corporations, teaching them how to use nature by making biology a natural part of the design process by seeing nature as "model, measure and mentor" and that we should learn "form, process and ecosystem level natural strategies. Biomimicry is basically taking a design challenge and then finding an ecosystem that's already solved that challenge and literally trying to emulate what you learn." She also says, "The conscious emulation of life's genius is a survival strategy for the human race, a path to a sustainable future." Go to End Notes to see her video on TED Talks.[1]

Ecologist and Writer Carl Safina explores the scientific, social, and moral dimensions of our relationship with nature. He dares to ask the question "Who are we here on Earth with? Who are you?" In his book *Beyond Words – What Animals Think and Feel* and in his TED and Google Talks, he makes a compelling case that animals experience the world in a similar way to us and have a very rich internal (thinking and feeling) and social experience and that they have consciousness, intelligence, rationality, creativity, empathy, and love. He says what makes us human is that we, as a species, are the most "extreme" because "we are the most compassionate, violent, creative and destructive that has existed on this planet." He says that we must ask ourselves, "Do we have enough: consciousness, intelligence, rationality, creativity, empathy, and love to let life on earth survive?" Please check out Carl's video; it will change you.[2]

To use this book successfully, you need to see your people, your business, and the world as a reflection of yourself. You will be asked to be honest with yourself and brave enough to turn inward, shine the light on things you or others don't like, and not look back. You must challenge your way of looking at the world. If you don't and just read this as an intellectual pursuit, it won't make a difference. This process is simple, but it will require keen awareness, sincere positive intention, not taking yourself so seriously, and, most of all, practice.

Get ready for a journey that leads you home to your real self, to a place of both deep connection and full individualistic self-expression. To get there, you'll need to let go of thoughts, feelings, limiting beliefs, and perceptions that separate you from feeling connected to others, make you rigid in your thinking, and stop you from being fully aware in the moment.

You'll have to be willing to believe that you can paradoxically achieve more by doing less. You'll relinquish force, stop overstriving, and instead, relax into your own internal knowing. You'll learn to work smarter, not harder. The Chinese have a saying "Rou overcomes gang," which means, **"Soft and flexible overcomes hard and energetic."**

The Way is about seeing ecosystems, honouring nature, becoming more conscious of our own human nature, and being sensitive and connected to everything and everyone around us. It is about developing products, systems, and ways of being that don't stress or pollute our Earth and its inhabitants. On September 10th, 2017, *BBC Business News* reported that China looks to ban gas and diesel cars, joining the UK and France who have already announced their plan to ban them by 2040. They also reported that Volvo will have electric engines in all their cars by 2019. Kudos to these leaders.[3]

Effective leaders continually learn and grow. This book encourages your self-awareness and self-cultivation and will provide you with insight into the areas of leadership development, culture creation, change management, conflict management, self-mastery, performance, and learning and development.

The Way of Effortless Leadership is different from other models. It places you as an integral part of the natural world, not separate or master of it. You get to use nature's force.

My hope is that you feel yourself return to something you may have lost some time ago: a fun, playful childlike sense of wonder, anticipation, and being at one with nature. Close the door, remove the

The Way of Effortless Leadership

serious adult cloak from around your shoulders, and use your imagination. Sit back in your most comfortable chair. Think back to a time when you were mesmerized, entranced, and taken over by the beauty of nature. Maybe you're lying on your back under a tree in the shade without a care in the world watching nature play its symphony. There might be a cool breeze caressing your skin, the smell of flowers, sounds of birds and bees, and the grass swaying in the wind. Maybe you're on a beach.

My tai chi chuan Master Eddie Wu Kwong Yu once told me that the health and martial aspects of tai chi chuan can't be separated because one first needs vibrant health to be able to do the martial, and practicing the martial helps one's health by protecting one's body. The same holds true for you and your people. You must put a premium on wellness because only when you and your people are physically and psychologically well, can energy, performance and productivity thrive. This is inside-out leadership.

The Way is much simpler and more paradoxical than you thought. You'll see that optimal performance requires optimal health, and optimal health requires integrating your body and your mind and realizing that your emotions and feelings are just as important as thinking. You'll discover that using your position, power, force, and control will work against you and that using awareness, intention, and trust will free you. You'll feel relaxed and revitalized, seeing and appreciating the power, efficiency, effectiveness, and beauty of nature's design. You'll understand that you must change yourself first before external results happen.

I believe that true leadership is about achieving and facilitating true wealth: life, growth, well-being, balance, self-expression, connection/love, and realization of potential. You'll learn how to self-cultivate or self-actualize and help your people to do the same.

Following the Way will make your life happier, empower your people, and help you achieve sustainable and effortless business results. My desire is that the Way helps you transform your teams and organizations into places where people feel truly alive, well, empowered, and inspired to give their best to each other so you can thrive together.

When you finish this book, you might say, "It is almost too simple," but I believe that in its simplicity lie its power, beauty, and the reason why it works. The only things that stand in your way are your ego, your attachment to things, and your unwillingness to be courageous and stand up for what is right.

> *"When your inner world comes into order, your outer world will come into order."* —I Ching

The Way of Effortless Leadership

PART TWO:
WHY THE WAY?

"A human being is part of the whole, called by us universe ... We experience ourselves, our thoughts and feelings as something separate from the rest. A kind of optical delusion of consciousness. This delusion is a kind of prison for us, restricting us to our personal desires and to affection for a few persons nearest to us. Our task must be to free ourselves from the prison by widening our circle of compassion to embrace all living creatures and the whole of nature in its beauty. The true value of a human being is determined by the measure and the sense in which they have obtained liberation from the self. We shall require a substantially new manner of thinking if humanity is to survive." —Albert Einstein

Chapter 3 – Why Aren't Things Working?

"The greatest enemy of knowledge is not ignorance; it is the illusion of knowledge." —Stephen Hawking

So, let's recap.

Look at almost any business goal. Why does most of what we create and do fail to inspire, engage, and produce the desired results?

The odds of your organizational change failing is worse than if you flipped a coin. Why does 70 – 85% of organizational change fail?

How many business goals are you meeting or exceeding? If you're meeting them, what are the costs to your people? What are the costs to you? What are the costs to the environment?

Why is it so difficult to get the best out of people?

I suggest that it's because we:

- Have been trying to motivate living biological beings with an outdated Newtonian mechanical model.

- Treat business as a machine that's separate from nature and the earth.

- Think our intellect is superior to nature's design.

- Don't consider how our actions will impact our larger systems. We focus on parts not wholes.

- See ourselves as consumers. We have unbridled greed and think that more money and possessions mean more happiness.

- Don't see human beings. We see workers, DOINGs, or cogs in a machine that need to be repaired, managed, manipulated, and controlled.

- See ourselves as separate from others.

- Look outside ourselves, to others to find the answers.

The Way of Effortless Leadership

- Have stopped being natural and rely on techniques.

- Work in the opposite direction of nature's way. A typical project management approach is to put the focus on having (Results), then Doing, and, finally, achieving a desired state of Being. But it should be reversed.

- Treat people as inherently flawed and largely incapable, and, therefore, micromanage them.

- Focus on our own identity, status, success, wealth, happiness, and reputation, which narrows our awareness of what's happening around us.

- Pretend that we have the answers when we don't.

- Are out of balance.

- Have negative, fearful, and aggressive thoughts that create negative vibrations within the culture.

- Think of everything as a competition with winners and losers.

- Lack compassion.

- Are impatient.

- Are harried, nonstop movers and DOERS, unable to see the forest for the trees.

- Hoard resources and communication for personal gain and team protection, instead of sharing them for the broader good.

- Rely on constantly changing leadership models, techniques, and procedures that prevent us from being present, aware, and seeing what's real.

- Are tense, rigid and inefficient, and not fluid and spontaneous.

- Aren't authentic.

- Complicate things.

- Use our position, fear, or force to control, and that creates resistance.

The Way of Effortless Leadership
Chapter 4 – What Is the Solution?

Do you remember George Costanza, played by Jason Alexander on the sitcom *Seinfeld?* If you don't, George was a character whose life didn't work on any level. He lived with his parents, couldn't get a good job, wasn't attractive to women, etc. There was one episode called "The Opposite" where Jerry says to George:

"If every instinct you have is wrong, then the opposite would have to be right."

The rest of the episode sees George live this mantra and everything from jobs to relationships turn around for him. He alters his beliefs, assumptions, and feelings about himself and what's possible. In turn, others feel the change in his energy; they treat him differently and everything works out effortlessly for him.

So, the Way encourages you to be a quiet rebel, be "Opposite George" and do the opposite of what failing leaders are doing:

1. Choose a new scientifically accurate quantum/string theory/neuroscience paradigm of the world.

2. Realize that you, your people, and nature are all intimately interconnected. Realize you are all BEINGS not DOINGS or merely consumers. Identify with our blue and green planet and the cosmos not dogmas, identities, or things that objectify and divide us.

3. See and appreciate the brilliance in nature's design. Don't try to outthink her. Observe and listen and let her inform your BEING, thoughts, feelings, and actions. See her as your mentor and the model of how to create sustainable healthy growth. Develop systems and products that mimic her way and use her design and forces. Get out of her way. See yourself as worthy and an integral part of her, not master over her.

4. Downshift your ego. Get out of your head. Get into your body. Open to more subtle awareness around you, and help your people do the same.

5. Stop the mindless nonstop doing. Build in time for quiet

reflection. Only through reflection can you and your people learn and grow.

6. Filter all business goals through the prism of supporting life, sustainable growth, and people's self-realization. Seek to do no harm to people and the environment. Put your attention on your people's experience and their growth.

7. Simplify.

8. Be patient. Nature has its course.

9. Ensure your BEING, behaviour, actions, and anything you design (culture, programs, policies etc.) align with human nature and really motivates and helps people learn and grow.

10. Don't get stuck on using any technique/program; doing so will make you lose awareness of reality and what's going on and make you rigid in your thinking and ability to respond.

11. Mimic nature. Follow her way:

    a. **BE**
    Focus on yourself first. See your BEING, your character as the seed.

    b. **DO**
    Plant this seed to grow a new culture, align everything you create, change, and do to fertilize and nurture this new learning and growth-oriented culture.

    c. **HAVE**
    Reap the RESULTS you want.

    d. **REFLECT**
    on what you've learned.

    e. **REPEAT**

The Way of Effortless Leadership

12. Use Wu Wei, nature's principle.

"I'm not worried about giving computers the ability to think like humans. I'm more concerned about people thinking like computers, without values and compassion…

When you keep people at the center of what you do, it can have an enormous impact." —Tim Cook, Apple CEO (Commencement speech at MIT 2017)

Chapter 5 – Why Choose Nature's Way?

"If you lose touch with nature you lose touch with humanity."
—Jiddu Krishnamurti

Why choose nature's way when other leadership models are available that operate outside of this paradigm?

BECAUSE:

- We're part of nature's holistic living system that's self-organizing and self-healing.

- We're biological beings that require biological not mechanical solutions.

- Nature's principles are simple, universal, and easy to grasp.

- It works because it's what your people want and need.

- Nature works 100% of the time. Other leadership change models fail most of the time because they're unnatural; don't work with human nature; and don't allow for naturalness, flexibility, and the unexpected. They slow down our responsiveness.

- You can't hold nature back. It's the most efficient, effective, and effortless growth and change system.

- It's healthy, doesn't pollute, and doesn't require struggle and strain.

- Business isn't a machine; it's made up of people who are all part of nature. Everything has a life cycle or life flow.

- It is easy to remember and teach because there are just a few simple principles to follow. Whenever you're in doubt, you just need to look out at nature to remember its way.

- Animating life force, qi, energy, flows within and through all things. Nothing is permanent except energy (it just changes form). Everything changes. For health and growth to occur naturally and in a balanced way, conditions must be right.

- Everything is an ecosystem. People are ecosystems that live within team ecosystems that live within the larger business ecosystem that lives within the larger societal ecosystem, and they all communicate back and forth. There's always another layer of the onion. When one part of an ecosystem changes, the whole changes (if only slightly). We as a personal human ecosystem have a human nature that requires certain conditions for optimal growth and performance. Organic systems are perfectly coordinated, sensitive, and responsive to change, and they regenerate themselves. They're energy-based, process-oriented, and operate on the flow and sharing of information.

- We're all intimately interconnected such that being compassionate and trying to remove the suffering of others isn't just being altruistic but is, ultimately, being kind to ourselves.

- We're one Body-Mind-Spirit. Our mind isn't superior or separate from the body. We're one whole and we operate holistically. Thinking and feeling is unified.

- It's more fun, easier, relaxing, and it leads to personal growth.

- **Nature's design is without rival, it combines** colour, sound, form, and function. It's predictable. Everything happens and flows in cycles. Following natural order leads to health, balance, and success.

- In nature, everything complements everything else and is in perfect balance. It's an ecosystem based on interdependence.

- It works on abundance. It doesn't hoard and isn't greedy. It uses what it needs and leaves the rest.

- It is effective by being perfectly relaxed, coordinated, and efficient.

- There's no waste. Everything is used. There's no pollution.

- **Everything is sacred simply because of its BEING or existence.** One tree isn't better than another or one species more important than another. Diversity and balance are nature's strength.

- **Movement is health in nature**. Free flowing conscious energy is the source of everything and animates all life. Like water in an ecosystem or blood in our body, energy communicates through interdependent networks like streams. When energy is blocked, things become rigid, break, and die. When water stops flowing, it becomes stagnant and breeds disease.

- It is perfectly balanced.

- There are clear patterns and a predictable seasonal order to growth, alternating dormant and active growth. Continuous observable growth is NOT possible or natural.

- Healthy life/youth has a strong, flexible, receptive, and free-flowing life force energy that survives strong winds of change.

- It's physically and mentally grounding.

- Everything in nature is what the Chinese call Zi Ran (self-so) and follows its own nature towards full self-expression and realization.

- Nature is change and transformation. Nature is paradoxical from a dualistic point of view but not so if seen through a holistic lens. Everything flows with change, not changing too much or too little but in sync. A tree neutralizes the wind's force by bending just enough, not more or less than it needs to.

- Nature is sensitive and responsive to change and conflict but doesn't overreact.

The Way of Effortless Leadership
Chapter 6 – We Are All Atmans

See Yourself and Your People as Sacred

Who do you think you and your people really are in the larger scheme of things? In Yogic understanding, people's real selves are not their independent egocentric personalities; they're "Atmans," souls who are born divine and are one and the same as the transcendent reality, "Brahman," Tao in Taoism, or Buddha Nature in Buddhism.

The terms in this book are mostly Chinese and come from Taoism. This chapter uses the term *Atman*, which comes from Indian/Hinduism/Yogic philosophy but Taoism's view of who people are in the scheme of things is in line with this concept. The words *divine* and *sacred* are used in the sense of being tied to nature, not the religious connotation. **The Way is the opposite of dogma**.

In the last few years, businesses have been having conversations about how employees should be treated. This is a step in the right direction. However, there hasn't been a deep conversation about who people are at their core.

Many organizations tout their "people first" culture, strategies, initiatives, and policies. Yes, the words *social responsibility, wellness, respect, diversity, work-life balance,* and *talent management* have entered the corporate lexicon. In Canada, we have legislation against bullying, yet there's more and more mental injury being reported at work. Why is that? What's happening?

Consider the current common saying, "People are our most valuable asset or resource." The line seems impressive, even progressive, right? **Do you and most leaders in your organization personally treat people that way?** Or, do you, like most, just use it as a line to recruit and tick off the social responsibility box to look good to your shareholders and the public so you can make more money? The words *asset* and *resource* make you think of accounting and production. Would you like to be treated like a thing, an asset, a resource to be used and managed? Is that who you are and how you want to be treated?

Newton Marguilies and Anthony Raia in their book *Organizational Development* listed two important values of Organizational

Development as "providing opportunities for people to function as human beings rather than resources in the productive process" and "treating each human being as a person with a complex set of needs, all of which are important to their work and their life."

To use nature's way, you must not only change how you see the world as interdependent and interconnected but **also shift your perception of who people are in relation to the world and each other.**

> **The universe is sacred.**
> **You cannot improve it.**
> **If you try to improve it, you will ruin it.**
> —*Tao Te Ching* (29), Lao Tzu

We've felt disconnected from ourselves, separate from others, and isolated and superior to nature. We've disembodied ourselves by identifying ourselves solely with our intellect. I believe the increase in mental injury is due to this feeling of alienation and a misperception of who we really are as beings.

Our focus has become more self-centered. Success is now defined as personal success. Wealth has been confused with money, which just represents wealth. People think they can isolate themselves and be materially successful while the rest of the natural world and others fail around them. Consumption, self-promotion, self-aggrandisement, and self-importance have become all important. I believe there's a better way.

Take a moment and think back to a time when someone treated you as a resource or asset to accomplish their goals. Now compare that to a time when someone saw and appreciated your being. Do you feel the difference? **Simply holding someone in your mind as being a whole and complete sentient being, a soul who's born divine versus perceiving him or her as a resource or asset to be used, will empower them.** This is about seeing someone's true self and potential and treating them as such.

An *asset* or a *resource* is a utilitarian business term for a tool to reach your goals. Do you treat your wife, father, daughter, or friend as an asset that helps you achieve a goal? No, you treat them as "Atmans." They're complex, special, dear, unique, and of value simply because they share your time on this planet. They're part of the richness of your experience of life, and their perceptions and feelings are

The Way of Effortless Leadership

important to you. You're tuned into them and their experiences of pain, fear, joy, and love. You wish the best for them and try to make their life richer and deeper, as they do you.

"What lies behind us and what lies before us are small matters compared to what lies within us." —Ralph Waldo Emerson

To succeed using the Way, start by feeling that you're part of nature and are sacred. Understand that you have a basic choice to approach people from a place of love and unity or fear and division. Appreciate each of your people as Atmans and expand your sensitivity and compassion for them before you design, introduce any initiative or policy, or do anything that will impact them. Just be with them without an agenda for a while. Turn your attention to understanding their experience. Doing so doesn't mean that you approve of all behaviour but that you see and appreciate the real self behind the behaviour. If you do, you'll cultivate sincerity and deep compassion and love that will be felt. You'll change your internal vibrations, which will be picked up by your people, and your culture will transform for the better.

Everyone behaves contrary to their better nature at times, but that doesn't mean that you must perceive their innate being differently. Everyone makes mistakes. You can separate the being from the behaviour. If you're required to have a difficult conversation with someone, holding them as if they were sacred will change how the individual receives the information because you've previously built a solid foundation of deep trust, respect, and appreciation of him or her.

"Love is a temple
Love a higher law
Love is a temple
Love the Higher Law…

One love
One blood
One life
You got to do what you should
One life
With each other
Sisters
Brothers

One life
But we're not the same
We got to carry each other
Carry each other
One"

Excerpts from "One" lyrics by Bono of U2

The Way of Effortless Leadership
Chapter 7 – The REAL "Real" World

We and everything in the universe operates on emptiness and vibration

Business leaders often talk about business as being the real world. This belief couldn't be further from the truth. Business has operated in a bubble outside the laws of nature, and that's why things don't work. It has been using an incomplete and outdated Newtonian model or understanding of the way the universe works.

This chapter goes into the theory of the nature of reality as explained by the current science and eastern philosophy or "mysticism." It's nature-based and the foundation of the "model" of the Way. I believe that this perennial philosophy, which has been around for thousands of years and is modelled on nature, has something profound to teach us. The Way is cosmological, ontological, ecological, and psychological. We need an accurate understanding or view of the universe or world, so that we can be and act in an appropriate way that works with it, and this will, in turn, allow us to be effective, achieve results, and be healthy.

I bring my experience as a Wu Style tai chi instructor and an avid yoga student to this chapter. Authentic tai chi Chuan is a powerful "soft" internal martial art: however, its final purpose as described in the *Chant of the Thirteen Kinetic Movements* is "Longevity with eternal spring," or to prolong life and well-being. This is true wealth. Internal martial artists, those who practice tai chi chuan, aikido, jujitsu, judo, systema (Russian martial art), use the Tao's/Way's principles of nature to adopt the "beginner's mind" and spontaneously harmonize and flow with the opponent. Their arts transcend technique and don't rely on it. Instead, they use awareness and become one with the opponent. They don't block force; they join with it, neutralize, and exhaust it. Softness wins by accepting and neutralizing the force, by leading it to the empty space where there's no balance. In the tai chi form, one begins and ends with stillness (Wu Chi). In between, one moves fluidly, continuously, like water, with no breaks in movement to achieve a state of flow. Using mental intention, relaxation, awareness, and coordinating one's breath with movement is part of the secret power of tai chi. The mind, the body, and the breath achieve a perfect state of coordination. When one part of the body-mind moves, the whole body-mind moves and changes one's internal vibrational energy or qi. I believe these are life lessons that can be very effective in business.

There's a relationship between consciousness (energy/nonmaterial) and matter (material) that's different from what we perceive, believe, and have been taught. Consciousness (flow of awareness, thought, sensation, emotion, interpretation, and intention) is primary and it gives rise to matter, not the other way around. Form or matter is temporary and energy is permanent. Remember high school physics. The First Law of Thermodynamics states, "Energy can neither be created nor destroyed, rather, it transforms from one form to another."

We know the world through our senses. Science and Eastern mysticism (Taoism and Hinduism) tell us that our sensory perception of reality is false, an illusion or "Maya." It's as if we're sleepwalking. This is like the movies *The Matrix* and *Avatar*. To access reality, we must temporarily turn off our externally directed sensory perception, tune into our internal experience through meditation and mindfulness, and wake up from our sleep.

"There is no matter as such. All matter originates and exists only by virtue of a force, which brings the particle of an atom to vibration and holds this minute solar system together. We must assure behind this force the existence of a conscious and intelligent mind. This mind is the matrix of all matter." —Max Planck, Quantum Physicist

Scientists know that the deeper they probe into reality, the less material and predictable it becomes. Ironically, the things that we can't directly perceive are more real than those we can. Paradoxically, the smaller the building blocks of reality, the more power they have to create or destroy (think of what happens when you split an atom – nuclear explosion). Beyond the level of the atom, it gets even stranger. There are only strings of vibrating energy and space/emptiness at the heart of reality. Everything is composed of atoms and atoms are composed of 99.9 % empty space. Even the smallest "material" particles are just space and tiny energy strings vibrating at different frequencies but they create the diversity of our material world. Everything in existence vibrates. Vibration is an energy that creates movement, life, and experience. Vibration creates various waves (sound, light, earthquake, etc.). Forces of energy hold our perceived reality together. White light, when put through a prism, breaks down into colours that we perceive. These colours have different vibrational waves that affect different energy centres or chakras in our bodies per yoga.

"Thirty spokes unite around one hub to make a wheel. It is the presence of the empty space that gives the function of a vehicle. Clay is molded into a vessel. It is the empty space that gives the function of a vessel Doors and windows are chiseled out to make a room. It is the empty space in the room that gives its function. Therefore, something substantial can be beneficial, while emptiness of void is what can be utilized." —Tao Te Ching (12), Lao Tzu

How do we understand and operate in the world? We're both receivers and transmitters of different forms of vibration/energy waves. We have five senses: sight, sound, taste, smell, and touch. These allow us to understand and interact with the world around us by interpreting energy or vibration in different ways. If you were to lose all of your senses, your experience of the outside world would disappear. Light and colour is energy made visible. Sound, energy made audible. Flavour, energy you can taste. Matter is energy you can touch. Scent is energy you can smell. Whereas, qi or chi energy which is life's battery is a subtle energy you can feel or experience internally and relates to what many call the sixth sense, intuition.

Taoists believe the true reality behind the illusion is **"The Tao,"** nature's way. Nature's way is about life and growth. Life grows from simple to complex. **Eastern philosophy is about reversing, returning to ultimate simplicity, to the source of life.** The Tao is beyond conceptualization because it's the totality of everything. No one can grasp its totality; one can only point to it. However, there are ways to experience it directly and I'll share some of those with you as we move through the book. Other Eastern spiritual traditions have similar views. Hindus call it "Brahman." Indigenous people call it "The Great Spirit." They believe we falsely see the world as physical or material and everything and everyone in it as separate and only interacting mechanistically. The limitations of our five senses block our ability to see that we're **one intelligent unified field of energy**.

The Tao (the way of nature or existence) has two basic expressions:
1. **Wu Chi: still** (outside Space-Time, pre-Big-Bang, containing no-things, a different dimension), empty, formless and unknowable expression of oneness that lacks identity. It can be likened to a still ocean of a mysterious potentiality fluid from which everything will be created in the next stage.

2. **Tai Chi: moving**, the constantly changing, dualistic world that we know that exists within space-time that creates distinction and identity. Yin (negatively charged) and yang (positively charged) are complementary opposite moving forces of the tao. Their movement creates waves within the normally still ocean of Wu Chi producing everything in our reality. Instead of thinking of yin and yang as separate opposites: "male" and female," "front" and "back," "up" and "down," "leading" and "following," "stillness" and "movement," "thinking" and "feeling," or "success" and "failure" etc., think of them as wholes: "front-back," up-down," "leading-following," "stillness-movement," "thinking-feeling," and "success-failure." This removes the duality and recognizes the interdependence of nature. One "opposite" must have the other to exist and there's always a bit (the seed) of one in the other. In fact, one cannot know one without knowing its opposite. Things and experiences are defined by their opposite. You can never know up without knowing down. The yin yang symbol is two fish chasing each other in a spiraling movement within a circle of emptiness (Wu Chi).

The Tao flows from Wu Chi (nonexistence/nothingness) to Tai Chi (existence/ everythingness) and then things return to Wu Chi (nonexistence/nothingness) in transformational waves, continuously repeating itself. We and everything else in existence are a microcosm of the Tao. We mirror its process. We don't exist, then our parents have a union (Big Bang), we're born, live an individual life wave, eventually falling back into the ocean of Wu Chi, nonexistence. Wu Chi, the Void, is particularly important, as it's the source of everything.

> *"Return is the movement of the Tao.*
> *Yielding is the way of the Tao.*
> *All things are born of being.*
> *Being is born of non-being."*
> —*Tao Te Ching,* 40, Lao Tzu

So, if we're just part of one large energy field, what becomes most important? Our internal vibrations and our relationships to each other. Learning to understand how the other is experiencing things and how we view and treat each other.

The Way of Effortless Leadership

The truth is that we're all one at the deepest level but also uniquely individual and differentiated superficially at the same time. This is incredibly important because this knowledge tells us who we are to each other. You're not a thing. You're a BEING. As discussed in the last chapter, **Yogic philosophy says we're part of this same flow of energy or spirit and are all "Atmans" (souls), born divine. Each moment is unique and sacred.** Yogis observed all living things and saw that being born (becoming conscious) must come before doing and doing must come before having. The idea is that unconditional love, compassion, and acceptance of the being changes the vibration and the relationship between two beings. In the same way, dogs sense each other's energy and intention. To flow with nature, we must wake up to this reality and treat each other in this way. If we don't start seeing each other as interconnected energetic beings, we won't be able to lead from a place that works.

Leaders who see themselves as separate from their people and the world fail to acknowledge what's real and the way the universe operates; therefore, their goals come from a faulty premise. The charismatic, aggressive, self-centered powerful leaders with big egos and myopic sights on profit and material success might entertain but they don't inspire us or bring out the best in us. Humble leaders who treat us as souls, enlist us in an exciting vision of a collaborative world, and bring out our own leadership capabilities do.

All these Eastern systems believe it's possible to see and go beyond the grand illusion, and get in flow with The Tao/nature's unified field of intelligence. In fact, all these systems believe that nature's energy, power, or force (qi, chi, ki, or prana) flows through everything and everyone. When we do transcend the illusion, we're completely absorbed in the moment; merge with a universal mind or consciousness; and experience a feeling of love, bliss, and joy. Hindus call this "samadhi." Athletes and tai chi practitioners call it "flow." In Chapter 11, you'll learn more about flow.

Taoists, Buddhists and yogis **seek to live lives of harmony and balance**. They see the universe as growth, consciousness, and being-oriented, not end-focused. Think about it; what's the purpose of your pet dog? What's the purpose of a tree? What's the purpose of an elephant? There's no purpose. They, like you, come into life with the purpose of experiencing life and to learn how to be in the world. Growth happens cyclically and through spirals. The Tao is the life principle, process, or way the universe works. Yogis believe meditation quiets the mind, silences our incessant thoughts, and allows us to get in flow with nature and access its subtle information and intelligence. Taoists and tai chi players use **yi, forceless intention to create.**

Awareness, sensitivity, imagination, and intention are powerful tools. Taoists, Buddhists, Yogis, and tai chi chuan masters use the **power of the mind and shun the overuse of force**. Everything that's created is first a thought in someone's mind and then one uses intention to materialize it. So, imagination and thought is much more powerful than force. We use the Reticular Activating System in our brain to choose our focus. This system determines what information is filtered out of our consciousness and what is allowed in. When we choose to be aware of certain things, feelings, and thoughts, we change our vibrations or frequency, which changes the way other people experience us, and that changes their behaviour and, in turn, our reality and results.

Taoists observed that the growth of the universe/nature is a self-organizing spiralling toroidal (donut-shaped) flow of energy. The centre point is zero point, singularity, or void. From the void (0), it grew and is continuing to grow in a sequence similar to Fibonacci's numbers (0, 1, 2, 3, 5, etc.), where the next number in the sequence is found by adding the two previous numbers.

In Taoism, creation of the cosmos can be explained in the following order:
- a) The Tao's original state was undifferentiated unity/precreation "Wu Chi" or The Void or "potentiality" in Aristotle's terms, or the number "0."
- b) Then came the first differentiation, qi, "1." This is the animating life force that has perfectly balanced and neutral energy.
- c) Then qi, the life force created "2" complementary/balancing opposing forces (yin/negatively charged and yang/positively charged) or polarity. This is like the binary code in computing where all complexity is created out of a combination of only simple 1's and 0's.
- d) Yin and yang plus qi are called "The Three Pure Ones." It helps to think of a battery upon which life operates and grows, with positive and negative poles and qi being the force between them. This dynamic started moving, spiraling outward to become tai chi ("the supreme

ultimate") or "actuality" in Aristotle's terms. These three forms of energy are also called "jing" (essence that's yin/earth energy), "qi" (neutral, balanced energy) and "shen" (spirit that's yang/heavenly or cosmic energy). Taoists use the three for health and personal evolution by cultivating and refining them, using internal energy alchemy.

e) The three pure ones led to "5 Phases/Elements/Seasons." These five are the phases of energy transformation.
f) From the Five Elements, everything else in the universe "Ten thousand things" were and are being created.

You will begin in Wu Chi, balance all opposite (yin and yang) thoughts and actions, cultivate your qi (life force energy) and character, and follow the seasonal cycle of growth. This will allow you to enter a natural state of Flow so you can lead from a place of authenticity and create in a healthful and sustainable way. Most importantly, in everything you do, you'll use nature's operating principle of Wu Wei.

Taoist Cosmology

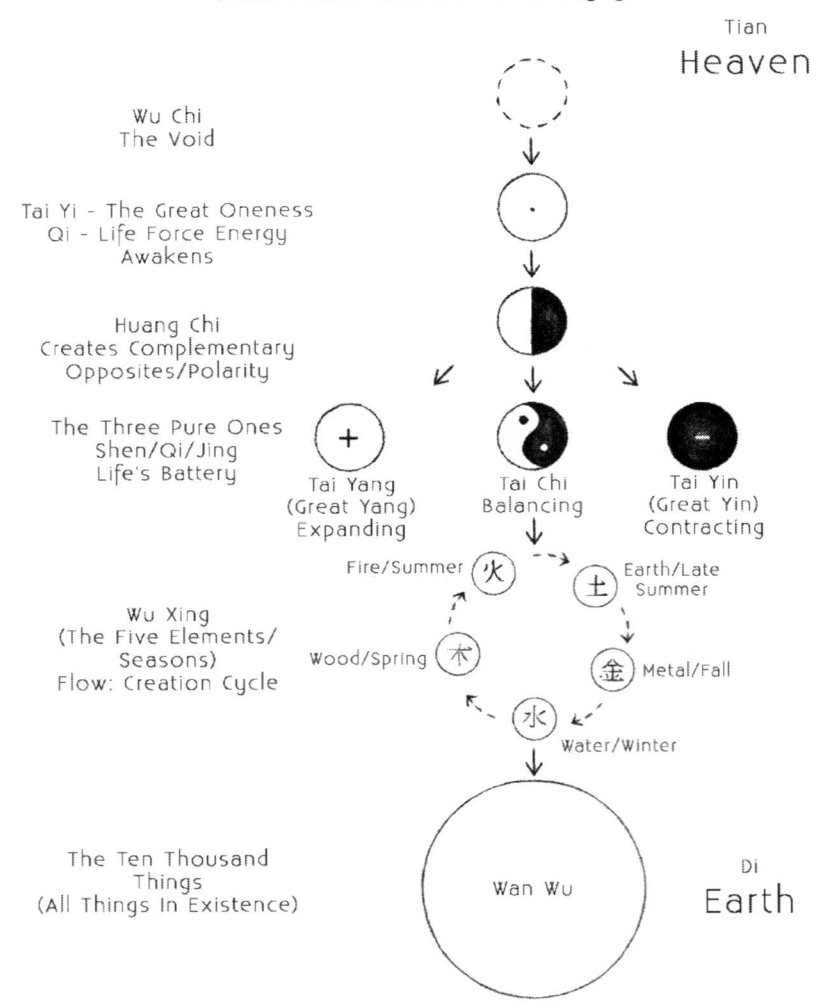

Tian
Heaven

Wu Chi
The Void

Tai Yi - The Great Oneness
Qi - Life Force Energy
Awakens

Huang Chi
Creates Complementary
Opposites/Polarity

The Three Pure Ones
Shen/Qi/Jing
Life's Battery

Tai Yang
(Great Yang)
Expanding

Tai Chi
Balancing

Tai Yin
(Great Yin)
Contracting

Fire/Summer

Earth/Late Summer

Wu Xing
(The Five Elements/
Seasons)
Flow: Creation Cycle

Wood/Spring

Metal/Fall

Water/Winter

The Ten Thousand
Things
(All Things In Existence)

Wan Wu

Di
Earth

Wu Chi is particularly important in the Way. It is prior to creation, outside space-time, and is really another dimension that can be accessed at any time and is always with us. It has unlimited potential and has the seed of all possibilities.

"We work with being, but non-being is what we use." –Lao Tzu

The new science supports this model.

The Way of Effortless Leadership

Niels Bohr, the famous physicist, who received the Nobel Prize for Physics in 1922 for his principle of "complementarity," traveled to China and studied Eastern philosophy. Jeffrey Stamps, in *Holonomy: A Human Systems Theory*, wrote,

> When Bohr was knighted for his achievements, he chose the symbol of tao for his coat of arms (Figure 5.1). In this symbol, writes Fritjof Capra (1975), "together with the inscription 'contraria sunt Complementa' (Opposites are Complementary), Niels Bohr acknowledged the profound harmony between ancient Eastern wisdom and modern Western science" (p. 100). (p. 46)

Top Quantum, Unified Field Physicists, and String Theorists have come to the same conclusion that in the beginning, there was a great unknown, undifferentiated, unified ONENESS they call the "Singularity." Then, the Big Bang happened and our universe was formed.

Famous Harvard quantum physicist John Hagelin believes that the Unified Field underlies all the forces of nature and is **"consciousness."** Hagelin practices Transcendental Meditation (TM). He agrees with the mystics that the Unified Field or what Taoists call The Tao (Wu Chi) or Hindus call Brahman is our REAL (nonlocal, nonego, potential) SELF and that it is accessible through meditation. In meditation, we still our mind so we can listen to and return to source, allowing us to get in flow with nature's way or design. Please watch John Hagelin's video on YouTube to learn how the universe uses vibration to create matter.[4]

Quantum physics informs us that the underlying reality is paradoxical and that we cannot be fully objective or removed from whom or what we observe. Our perception, our mind, our attention, and our intention changes "reality." Reality's default setting is that of waves (nonmaterial) and only becomes "material" when we (human consciousness) observe it with our sensory perception or instruments, as proved in double-slit experiments over the last hundred years. It is one interdependent process. **We're not separate beings. Everything we do affects the other (in small ways) no matter how far apart in space ("entanglement")**. So, as we discussed in the last chapter, We Are All Atmans, how you choose to perceive your people is how they show up to you.

Watch these videos; they explain this science clearly:

Parallel Universes and how to change reality[5]
Dr Quantum - Double Slit Experiment[6]

Famous Unified String Theorist Michio Kaku says in one of his YouTube videos *The Universe in a Nutshell,* that String Theory is a "theory of everything." Kaku says, "The **universe operates like music, with vibrating strings of energy**." Watch Michio Kaku's videos.[7]

Epigeneticist, Bruce Lipton, bridges the gap between science and spirit in his YouTube video *Epigenetics: The Science of Human Empowerment.* He says that we aren't "biochemical machines controlled by our genes." Your perceptions, thoughts, emotions, feelings, wishes, desires, and intentions change the environmental signals which change the "culture medium" (our blood composition), which, in turn, works to change your body's RNA and DNA. Watch Bruce Lipton's video.[8]

Taoist and Yogic belief in the power of intention is scientifically backed by this discovery. In a similar way, by shifting your being (vibrations and intention), you can be the signal that changes your organization's culture's medium or lifeblood.

Scientists know the universe is expanding and is continuing to grow at a predictable and increasing rate. Evolution is a learning and growth process towards higher and more complex states of being, awareness, and consciousness. Change and growth happen through repeating wave-like cycles of going from "Wu" (NON-BEING) to "Yu" (BEING) to "Wu" (NON-BEING), then transforming into something new, and repeating the process.

So, if the universe has a conscious, intelligent, intentional mind, and plays tiny strings of energy to create and evolve, why can't we use the same process?

In fact, many Eastern and Western traditions do just that. Practitioners use or change their own vibration to get in tune with nature to attain higher states of consciousness and dimensions through meditation, silent mantras, chanting, singing, drumming, and plant medicine. By recognizing or observing our thinking, emotions and turning off our opinionated dualistic world for a few minutes and tuning into nature's unity or oneness, we're able to grasp new insights and possibilities that we otherwise wouldn't have seen.

The Way of Effortless Leadership

"Music in the soul can be heard by the universe." —Lao Tzu

Remember, as a new paradigm leader, you're a talented musician who plays an inspiring and catchy tune that moves your people.

So, our observation, attention, and intention literally change our reality and make us more evolved.

SUMMARY KEY LESSONS FROM REALITY/NATURE:
1. Nature is elegantly simple at its deepest level.
2. We are one.
3. Returning to The Void or Wu Chi and changing our vibrations/frequencies is the deepest, simplest, and most effective way to get in sync with nature.
4. We change vibrations by meditating, being in nature, being sensitive, listening and expanding our awareness, and changing our thinking, feeling, and perception.
5. We influence "others" by paying attention to them and using our intention.
6. It's best to find the middle ground in all our actions and balance all complementary "opposites," especially stillness/inaction and movement/action, and thinking and feeling.
7. Intervening less and using conscious noncontrived or forceless action is the key to allow you to harness nature's way/ power.
8. Use natural cycles/waves to create, breakdown, transform, and evolve.

"Luminous beings are we. Not this crude matter." Yoda

Chapter 8 – Your Life Lens

"It is futile to put personality ahead of character, to try to improve relationships with others before improving ourselves." —Stephen Covey

Taoists and yogis view you as a microcosm or reflection of the world and cosmos. To influence the macrocosm/outer world, you must change yourself.

Before looking at the "model" of the Way, please take some time to reflect on your own life experience, perception, and values by completing the following self-assessment exercises. Your answers will be necessary for you to be able to use the Way.

1. Complete "My Life Balance Wheel." Evaluate your satisfaction and success in all areas of your life. Blacken in the appropriate amount of each pie slice, starting at the hub/center. If you're fully satisfied in a particular area of your life color in the whole slice. See where you're out of balance in your life. Balance is the key to true happiness and wellness.

The Way of Effortless Leadership

My Life Balance Wheel

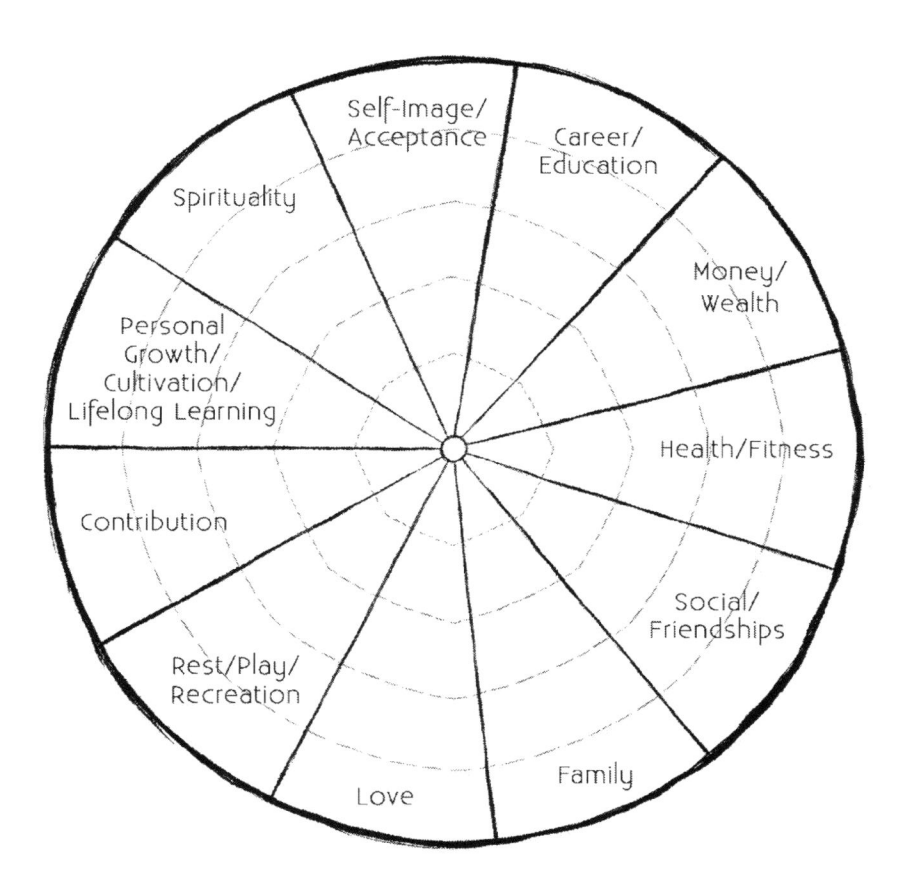

- Self-Image/Acceptance
- Career/Education
- Spirituality
- Money/Wealth
- Personal Growth/Cultivation/Lifelong Learning
- Health/Fitness
- Contribution
- Social/Friendships
- Rest/Play/Recreation
- Family
- Love

2. Complete Leadership Hopes vs. Leadership Reality Exercise

Close your eyes. Think back. What difference did you want to make to people, to your family, your community, the world before you became a leader? How did you imagine being the boss/leader would be like?

What were you looking forward to experiencing, doing, and achieving?

How are those thoughts different from your reality? Write down your thoughts, feeling, and realizations under the appropriate headings.

The Way of Effortless Leadership

Leadership Vision/Dreams/Hopes	Leadership Reality

3. Complete Best vs. Worst Bosses I've Had Exercise

Compare and contrast how you would describe the best and worst bosses you've had in your life. Compare how productive you were with each. How loyal you were to each. How you felt about yourself, the team, and the organization in their presence. See their faces, voices, mannerisms, and ongoing behaviour, values, etc.

Best Bosses/Leaders I've Had	Worst Bosses/Leaders I've Had

4. Complete How Do I Compare Exercise

Lastly, and this is the hard part, it requires complete honesty and willingness to be vulnerable. Compare your qualities and how you are with your employees as compared to the best and worst bosses you've had. You might be different with different people, so please make note of that.

The Way of Effortless Leadership

Best/Worst Boss Leadership Qualities	My Reality as a Leader

5. Complete Sentences

Complete the sentence stems to uncover your present view of people and the world. Don't second-guess yourself; just write down what first comes to you. After you've completed everything, look for trends in your thinking.

Life and Change
1. Life is about

2. Change means
3. The world operates on
4. Winners are
5. Losers are
6. Being controlling means
7. Success takes
8. My success requires your

Me/My Identity
1. _____ makes me feel unbalanced or ungrounded
2. If I make a mistake, my people will think I
3. I'd describe the vibes/energy I give off as being_____ and it makes people feel_____
4. People say I'm blind to _____ within myself
5. When I am stressed, I
6. _____ negatively triggers me
7. My biggest weakness or internal challenge is
8. I want to cultivate within myself the following qualities:
9. Letting go of control at work means
10. If I had all the money in the world, I would be different in the following ways
11. My identity is strongly tied to
12. I'm afraid my people will discover that I'm
13. I feel threatened when people challenge my
14. My nature is
15. My tendency to _____ interferes with my success
16. I get stubborn, rigid, and unable to accept new information when
17. At work, I generally feel
18. I'm judgmental of people who
19. I get negatively hooked or triggered when
20. I expect
21. I was brought up to believe
22. The qualities I admire the most are
23. I have become successful by
24. People see me as

The Way of Effortless Leadership

25. For me to succeed, you must

Work/Business Culture
1. The best work culture is
2. The business world is
3. My organization's culture makes me feel
4. My team is
5. Managing people's work is
6. Showing compassion at work is
7. Using fear and control at work
8. Simplicity at work is
9. Patience at work is
10. Fun and humour at work is
11. In business, I must
12. The unspoken rules to succeeding in our culture are
13. In our organization, thinking differently is
14. The three words that really describe our culture are
15. Giving people downtime to play and reflect at work

Leaders/Bosses
1. Leadership is about
2. People want a leader who
3. A boss who is feared is
4. A boss who is well liked is
5. People follow leaders who
6. A leader's job is to

People/Engagement
1. People leave organizations because of
2. I believe successful people
3. To innovate, people need
4. The single biggest thing that affects people's engagement and productivity is
5. Most people are
6. People who don't work hard but work smarter (and leave early) are
7. People need_____ to be productive
8. A subordinate's job is to
9. People who play at work
10. If I don't drive my people they will
11. If my people were successful and said, "We did it ourselves," (without giving you credit) I would

12. Employees who are constantly busy and work longer hours than most are

13. Seeing one of my employees closing their eyes or taking time out of their day to go for a walk outside would make me

14. People are inspired by

15. To lose self-concern and serve clients/customers well, people require

Now, read over your answers and summarize in a few sentences what you learned. Choose a few things to cultivate/change that you think will change you positively.

6. Antenna Up - Culture Audit

Your five senses and your intuition are valuable allies.

The purpose of this exercise is to see and feel afresh. Pretend you've never been into your company, and see and feel from that lens.

1. Still and clear your mind.

2. Be aware of your prejudices and biases towards people and departments and dissolve them for this exercise.

3. Take time to tune into the spirit, sound, feel, and dynamics of your team/organization. But, before you do, create the intention that you won't get hooked or caught up in the drama or business fires of the moment. Create the intention that you'll be still and just notice, and that you'll use what you discover for the benefit of everyone in your organization.

4. Walk about and take in the big picture. Do you see colour, life, movement, and flexibility, or do you see black and white, rigidity, and lack of movement? See your team or the organization as a whole ecosystem. Observe, listen intently, and notice the interactions or lack thereof. What is the vibration in the place? Do people's faces look relaxed and engaged or stressed and distracted? Is there a lot of laughter and open body posture or quiet tension? Are people hiding in the offices with heads down doing everything by email or up

The Way of Effortless Leadership

moving around and talking with people in different departments? Do people look and sound happy or anxious? Write down your observations.

5. If you're working in IT and dealing virtually with people, make time to use Skype and other face-to-face technology in order to keep the human connection.

6. Don't do anything with the information yet, just collect it.

7. Write down your impressions. Don't ascribe blame.

**PART THREE:
THE "MODEL" OF THE WAY**

Chapter 9 – The Way of Effortless Leadership "Model"

"Just stay at the centre of the circle and let all things take their course." —Tao Te Ching (19), Lao Tzu

Before you look at the graphic "Model" on the following page, use these suggestions to get the most out of it.

1. You are the person in the center of the "model" maintaining **Zhong Din** dynamic centered stability, awareness, and stillness through all the change and emotion. Be aware of your qi energy, thoughts, perceptions, and feelings. **Balance yin and yang** (i.e., reflection and action).
2. Your people are represented by the tree person in the model. See them as sentient **"Atmans"** (whole souls born divine and having a Buddha Nature) whose experiences of life are of most importance.
3. Forego the use of force, struggle, and strain. Use what the Chinese call your **yi (nonforceful intention/energy).**

The 3 Part "Model"

1) **Use nature's key principle, Wu Wei, effortless effort** or forceless action to achieve your goals. Use minimal energy and simple thoughts, actions, and language. Maintain a relaxed body and calm mind.

2) **Meditate to reconnect with nature's way, the Tao/Wu Chi (The Void or Nature's Source**) to stabilize, center, and empty your mind and tap into its force and intelligence.

3) **Do Leadership tai chi by flowing with the cyclical (order) of nature's five seasons** to achieve sustainable growth. Maintain awareness and a clear relaxed intention of your vision.

The Way of Effortless Leadership

1. USE WU WEI/EFFORTLESS ACTION
↓
2. RETURN TO WU CHI/ THE VOID

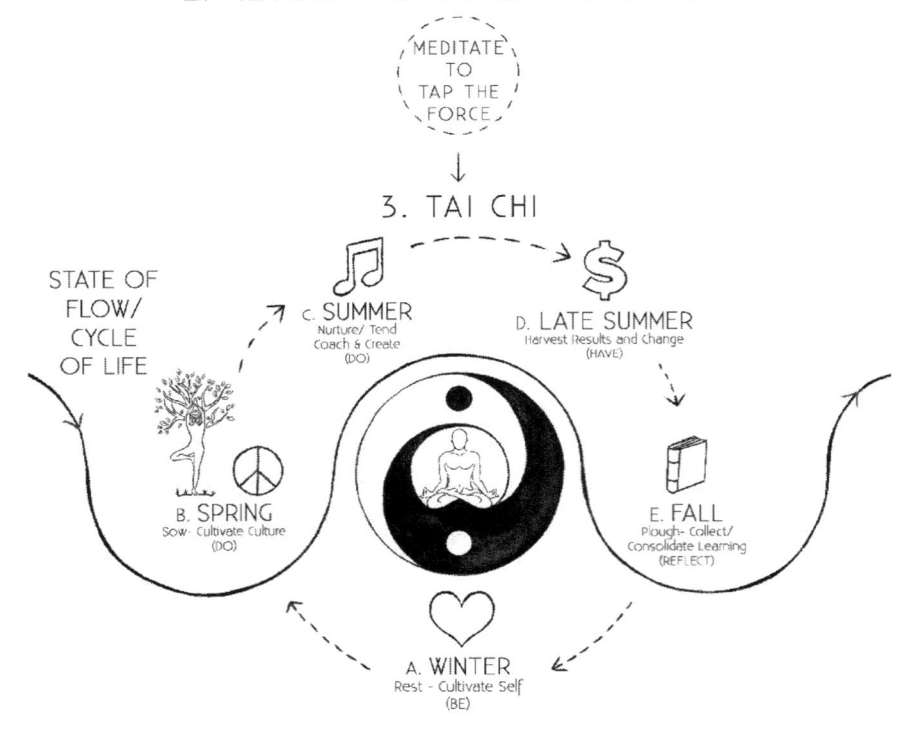

MEDITATE TO TAP THE FORCE

↓

3. TAI CHI

STATE OF FLOW/ CYCLE OF LIFE

C. SUMMER
Nurture/ Tend
Coach & Create
(DO)

D. LATE SUMMER
Harvest Results and Change
(HAVE)

B. SPRING
Sow- Cultivate Culture
(DO)

E. FALL
Plough- Collect/
Consolidate Learning
(REFLECT)

A. WINTER
Rest - Cultivate Self
(BE)

The Way of Effortless Leadership
Part 1 – Use Wu Wei

"For every action, there is an equal and opposite reaction."
—Newton's Third Law

If you get only one takeaway from this book, please let it be this one. **This principle of Wu Wei is the way nature works per Taoism. Please earmark this chapter and revisit it frequently.** Wu Wei is the opposite of using mental and physical struggle, strain, and force.

This principle is called Wu Wei (pronounced Wooo Way), which translates to "effortless effort," "forceless action," or "spontaneous action." You must use Wu Wei to follow and get in flow with nature and follow the Tao.

If you want your people not to buy into what you're doing, push them and tell them what to do. People hate to be told what to do. Just think about it. If I pushed you hard, how would you react? Most people push back and resist, setting up a battle between you and them. Look at your own experience. When was the last time someone used too much effort on you and tried to force, bully, or manipulate you to do something? Did you go along willingly? You either actively or passively resisted, or you walked away. If it was your boss, you may have had to go along, but you became suspicious and lost trust and respect for her and this trust was hard to regain. Your people will react the same way if you use force or manipulation on them.

Nature never uses more energy, material, or effort than is required. It's relaxed and accomplishes everything with the minimal amount of effort, maximum efficiency, and without overdoing or striving. Water runs downhill. Taoists noticed that nature operates on this principle.

It's about using nature's design and forces as opposed to using intellect, excess muscle, chemicals, or force to go against them. For example, I discovered that using a fan to mirror the wind to blow mosquitos away works much better than poisonous bug repellent. I noticed that deer venturing into our property would find the path of least resistance. When I cleared some paths, they chose to use them instead of their usual way through the forest. Wu Wei is about making your life easier. Paddling hard upstream against the flow of the river is the opposite of Wu Wei. In sailing a boat, adjusting sails and capturing the wind uses Wu Wei. Chopping wood with the grain (as opposed to against) uses Wu Wei. Surfing uses Wu Wei. Solar and wind power is Wu Wei, whereas fracking the earth to extract gas is not. Bungee jumping uses gravity, so does Wu Wei. Nature is perfectly secure and is continually improving and evolving.

What do you and others say about someone who's a master of any skill? **"They make it look so effortless."** Effortlessness isn't just something for the gifted; it's something that you can consciously cultivate within yourself, and is a key principle of the Way.

Your complex bodily systems, when healthy, work in harmony and effortlessly without struggle, strain, or having to think or force. One system doesn't try to compete, win, or overpower another. If one does become out of sync with the others, your whole organism gets sick and starts to break down. Coordination and an even and orderly flow are crucial.

To have an experience of effortlessness, put your hand on your chest and feel your heart beat that circulates the blood throughout your body to nourish it. Put your hand beneath your nose. Feel the continuous flow of air entering and exiting your body. The trees provide oxygen for you and you breathe out carbon dioxide for them in a symbiotic relationship. Your body has vital life force flowing through it and is continually exchanging energy, information, and nutrients with the outside environment to keep you alive. Plant chlorophyll is almost identical in structure to our body's hemoglobin. They are both composed of carbon, hydrogen, oxygen, and nitrogen but chlorophyll has a magnesium center while hemoglobin has an iron center. Interestingly, when we consume chlorophyll, it does the job of hemoglobin. It has the effect of improving the flow of circulation and increases red blood cell count, increasing the oxygenation of our body.

There are no silos in ecosystems. Your body is an ecosystem living within a larger ecosystem. Think about how this applies to your organization. You are an ecosystem within your team's ecosystem. Your team is an ecosystem within your organization's ecosystem. Your organization is an ecosystem within your community's ecosystem. Your community is an ecosystem within your state's ecosystem. Your state is an ecosystem within your country's ecosystem. Your country is an ecosystem within the world's ecosystem, etc. You are the microcosm of everything around you.

The Way of Effortless Leadership

My favourite bosses (Richard, Charlotte, and Frank) used Wu Wei without knowing they were doing so. If you observed them, they looked relaxed and still, as if they weren't DOING anything. Their way of BEING was what differentiated them. They tapped and leveraged everyone's creative energy and desire to make a difference by creating a safe and dynamic atmosphere. Teams worked in a coordinated manner. There was no or very little organizational silence and gossip in these workplaces and there was a very high degree of engagement, satisfaction, and performance. They never came on strong or forced ideas, points of view, or initiatives. They said little, listened deeply, and always sought to clarify and simplify. They created a wonderful employee experience that inspired me and others to give our all. They asked for and followed my/our ideas, flowing with what was important to staff. They operated in the background most of the time, which demonstrated a high degree of trust in me/us. They encouraged people to be themselves and voice their ideas and concerns without fear of reprisal. They were still, relaxed, compassionate, listened well, and maintained perspective and a great sense of humour in the most difficult times. I always felt they had my back, best interests, and personal growth in mind. They were always appreciative and gave away credit. They protected and nurtured the culture.

Wu Wei is such a simple principle but it requires deep relaxation, egoless and nonjudgmental awareness, great sensitivity, and the confidence to be present and go with the flow. Using Wu Wei requires that you:
- Suspend judgment and, with acceptance, take in everything around you
- Don't act until the timing is right
- Model, don't tell
- Get people excited by sharing an inspirational vision that they'll want to be part of
- Maintain balanced, neutral, peaceful energy
- Don't pretend
- Be humble
- Listen to learn and understand
- Use soft communication style
- Yield, as "soft overcomes hard"
- Simplify
- Facilitate group process
- Use simple noncontrived action
- Use noninterference. Do as little as needed

- Don't force your ideas, initiatives, or opinions
- Join with external force; flow with it
- Not seek acknowledgement and fanfare
- Use awareness
- Use sensitivity
- Use relaxed intention
- Use efficient movement
- Use leverage
- Look at systems and unintended consequences
- Coordinate all parts to create the gentlest of touch to effect change
- Use yi, clear relaxed mental intention, not hard concentration

It's not laziness. It's a fine line between doing too little and too much and each situation is different and requires your keen awareness and deep sensitivity. When you operate with Wu Wei, it allows your internal energy to flow freely and healthfully.

One company I went into epitomized the opposite of Wu Wei. It was a hard-driving culture. The first time I walked into the building, the silence was deafening. The company was simultaneously introducing multiple major change initiatives and there was virtually no buy-in because previous change initiatives had failed to take hold and inspire. Every time a new initiative was announced, people laughed, rolled their eyes, and sighed. No one spoke up and spoke their truth because it was a culture where organizational silence reigned because the leader branded people "whiners" and disagreement wasn't tolerated. People were admonished and let go if they didn't get on board. People came to me in droves, complaining about the culture of fear and silos that had been created by leadership. The organization was trying to "get ahead of change" but was overreacting and doing too much, too soon, forcing change, and not being sensitive and listening to their people's energy, emotional pain, and burnout. Their use of force damaged people's belief in the leadership, the culture, and each other. People were skilled and competent but were held back from excelling because of the culture of force and no trust. There was a lot of atomised DOING that failed to produce collaboration and results. No attention was paid to the quality of BEING, relationships, or culture. Leadership discouraged people from taking time to talk with other departments. People told me they always used email instead of meeting in person or talking on the phone as a way of "covering their ass" in case there was a dispute

The Way of Effortless Leadership

and it came back to haunt them. People turned inward and put all their energy into self-protection.

Humans try to impose their will on nature but our best results come when we flow with it. It's counterintuitive but works. It's the essence of systems thinking. Before you do, create, or say anything, pause and consider what might be some unintended consequences to other people, teams, and systems.

Effortless effort or forceless action doesn't mean complete absence of effort or action but requires engagement, awareness, intention, and the bare amount of energy to accomplish or leverage the task. There's a tai chi saying, "Four ounces can move 1,000 lbs." Top soft martial artists can use a finger to subtly offset an opponent who's already leaning slightly to one side. The martial artist relaxes and coordinates all his body to take the opponent in the direction he's leaning, using that person's energy and momentum and conserving his own. The more gently you move someone, the less chance the other person will tense up and put up resistance. The same holds true in business.

Think how much easier it is to take a raft in the direction of the river's flow. You paddle and steer to avoid rocks but you're using the natural flow of water to get where you're going. A good leader is like the rudder at the back of a boat. Its slight turn changes the course of the boat and can take it anywhere. She puts her people first.

What do you do well? A sport, a musical instrument, a game, an activity, a hobby, a discipline, or something else? A high level of proficiency or mastery requires a large degree of bodily relaxation and mental calmness. Relaxation opens your awareness, which allows you to see and react to distinctions that others don't see. It also allows you to be creative.

Todd Hargrove in his article "The Skill of Relaxation" wrote:

> If coordination means all the right muscles firing at the right time, this also means that any muscles *not* involved in the movement must relax in the right places at the right speed at the right time. Therefore, any act of coordination requires the skill of relaxing the muscles that aren't essential to the movement. If the nonessential muscles aren't relaxed, they will cause extraneous movement or tension that interferes in the desired movement and wastes energy.

Relaxing and coordinating the body (structure, muscles, bones, tendons, etc.) and aligning and stilling the mind are key to using the efficient power of tai chi. Through practice, you learn to differentiate between yin and yang "full" and "empty" or "active" and "nonactive" parts of the body. As you move a part that was active, it becomes inactive and vice versa. So, your whole body-mind-spirit work as one relaxed, fluid, coordinated efficient whole to achieve your "goal" with nothing working against it.

A ten-year-old high-level junior tennis player can hit the ball with much more power and accuracy than a fit, muscular man who's a beginner. The junior does this by relaxing his body right to the point of contact with the ball, then tenses a few muscles slightly, followed by complete relaxation. Yes, the ten-year-old uses some physical and mental effort but much less than the man. The child's body is relaxed, its structure and muscles work as one fluid coordinated whole, guided by the hip to strike the ball. The novice man will exert more muscular force than is needed. His muscles don't know how to relax and tense in the perfect order, so they work against each other. He tries to use force but uses mostly his arm, shoulder, and back muscles and not his whole body. In fact, his attempt at muscling the ball gets in the way of generating soft, fluid power. The man is unnecessarily tense and his body doesn't work as a fluid unified and relaxed whole. The man will quickly tire himself out physically and mentally because of the unnecessary tension in his body. The ten-year-old is efficient and effective by using his relaxed, coordinated effortless effort, and can play all day.

Like the mastery of anything, learning not to use muscle, force, and power will take time. Our society rewards neurotic forceful effort, especially in business. It will take commitment, discipline, practice, and awareness to use Wu Wei.

In relation to the concept of yin and yang, Wu Wei is more yin or soft. Remember, soft and relaxed overcomes hard and tense. Less is more.

Jon Kabat-Zinn, PhD, professor of medicine at University of Massachusetts Medical School, and Zen Buddhist meditation author, describes a similar Zen concept of "Non-Doing" is his book *Wherever You Go, There You Are:*

The Way of Effortless Leadership

"The inward stillness of the doer merges with the outward activity to such an extent that the action does itself. Effortless activity. Nothing is forced."

- Stay aware of how much effort you're expending.
- Is your body relaxed or tense?
- Are you putting in too much mental effort?
- Is your mind still or distracted?
- Are you tired?

If you're expending a lot of energy and constantly DOING, ask yourself why. Much of the time, your ego is getting in the way. Are you trying to look good? Are you avoiding looking bad? Are you trying to avoid someone getting the best of you? Are you trying to get the best of someone else? These are all forms of unnecessary attachment. If you notice that you're doing something to prove your worth and not for the real benefit of your people, stop it.

People want your real, sincere presence and for you to be relaxed. If you give them your trust, attention, heart, and positive intention to help them grow, they'll give you their heart and energy. Your results will improve because you will have provided a head, heart, and gut friendly climate that will bring out their own motivation. When people are intrinsically motivated, they become more committed and work harder because they feel they're co-creators and are invested in the outcome.

There are times when the appropriate thing is to use more energy and be a bit more forceful, but be aware of your intention and make sure it's appropriate to the situation and not an overreaction. Are your actions really in the best interests of your people or just to improve your image, career, or embellish your ego? Have you looked at the problem holistically or are you fixated on small parts?

Your simple, sincere, egoless, compassionate, well-intentioned, imperfect self is what your people want from you. Take time to just BE with them and listen to their ideas. Bring out the best in your people and they'll give you their best.

Ironically, if you're present and act selflessly for your people, there's a much greater likelihood of them sensing your authenticity, and your reputation/image and career goals will have a better chance of succeeding. However, again, don't strive for this goal; remain detached and just be and act without expectation.

Force creates an equal and opposite reaction. So, the leader who relinquishes force, trusts others, and uses minimal effort to accomplish his or her goals won't encounter the usual resistance or backlash from others.

- Keep an expanded awareness, a relaxed body, a calm mind, and use the minimal amount of effort to accomplish your goals.
- Maintain a still, relaxed, open, and neutral energy.
- Don't force your ideas.
- If you're stressed, take a few minutes and put your attention on your breath, sinking it to two inches below your belly button (the lower dan tien). If you can, meditate, stretch, or get outside into nature.
- Use a soft communication style; seek to listen and understand first.
- Don't overwhelm your people with too much. Too many initiatives that fail will damage the culture. The less intervention the better.
- Drop hard expectations.
- Don't focus on personal interests.
- Let go of need for fame and recognition.
- Trust your people and let the process take its course.
- Chill. Be patient.
- Smile.
- Maintain a sense of humour.

Stay still, step back, and your people will step forward. The more your products, programs and initiatives fit with nature's forces and design and human nature, the more your people will feel connected to them and ensure they take hold.

> **"The Tao nourishes by not forcing.**
> **By not dominating, the Master leads."**
> —*Tao Te Ching*, (81) Lao Tzu

The Way of Effortless Leadership
Part 2 - Return to Wu Chi (The Void)

Clear Your Mind

"Empty your mind; be formless, shapeless, like water. Now you put water in a cup, it becomes the cup. When you put water in a bottle, it becomes the bottle. When you put water in a teapot, it becomes the teapot. Water can flow and it can crash. Be water my friend."
—Bruce Lee

Sages for thousands of years have gone into nature and retreated into caves. They shut off external stimuli from their five senses and empty their minds to observe and transcend their thinking and connect to nature's way and experience the power and source of nature. They gained insights into life, leadership, and themselves by returning to the Wu Chi (the Void, the Singularity, or what Aristotle called Potentiality). This is a different dimension, as it is beyond the dualistic space-time constraints of everyday material existence. Wu Chi can be compared to an artist's blank canvas. It allows you to go beyond the veil to experience reality directly. It is both NON-BEING/nothingness and limitless creative potential. Everything is possible because nothing has begun. It is a dimension beyond the dualistic changing world of opinions and right and wrong. It allows you to experience nonstriving and nonbiased awareness. It is restful and will clear you mind. Returning to Wu Chi is the key part of accessing The Way or The Tao (nature's way) because when one is still, it's easier to sense it.

"Humans must achieve the ultimate void and maintain calmness with sincerity in order to observe the growth and flourish of all beings."
—<u>Tao Te Ching</u> (76), Lao Tzu

Most people identify themselves with their thoughts, feelings, ideas, beliefs, nationalities, religions, tribes, perspectives, and positions. Think about yourself being on one side of an issue and another person the other side. Whose position is right? You can only perceive what's happening around you and the other person can only see what is happening around them. To be able to grasp the totality of what is happening, you must temporarily suspend your perspectives and positions and go beyond duality, let go of your agenda and identify with the cosmos to see truth/reality. Returning to Wu Chi allows you to do so and see afresh.

> *"Empty your mind of all thoughts.*
> *Let your heart be at peace.*
> *Watch the turmoil of beings.*
> *But contemplate their return."*
> —*Tao Te Ching* (16), Lao Tzu

Business is usually a whirlwind of constant DOING. Business is confused with busyness. There isn't much time for rest, nondoing, and nonthinking. Dedicating time and space for people to do nothing is something that most business leaders would laugh at because it appears to the untrained eye as lazy and slacking off. However, wouldn't you agree that much of the work we do is unfocused, inefficient, and ineffective? DOING is **falsely seen as synonymous** with productivity.

The Chinese refer to our "monkey mind," as our emotional mind that jumps uncontrolled from one thing to the next. Returning to Wu Chi is about stilling the mind's chatter. Returning to Wu Chi is a source of rejuvenation and peace and it allows you to recenter, reset, ground yourself, and just BE. It also changes your vibration to one that harmonizes with nature.

The Chinese know that the mind-body connection is real and that when the mind is calm, the body relaxes and vice versa. It's about turning off the outside world, turning inward, and listening to and connecting with the Tao, in its simple unified formless form. It's the Wu Chi the source of energy that pulsates through all life. Return to Wu Chi whenever you need a break from the madness to ground yourself.

> *"The Void (Wu Chi), the state of empty, clear mindedness, remains both the goal and the source of practice. We don't achieve the Void, we 'return' to it. The Void is your original mind, an inner purity that has never been clouded by concepts and images."*

"An empty mind can sense internal blockages to the flow of qi (chi)…" —Kenneth S. Cohen - *The Way of Qigong*

The Way of Effortless Leadership

In *Star Wars,* Yoda trained Luke Skywalker in the forest surrounded by nature and taught him how to shut off his senses to access the Force. Wu Chi can be compared to what *Star Wars* calls "the force."

Science tells us our universe is ninety plus percent invisible dark matter and dark energy. This empty space-time isn't really empty; scientists just don't know exactly what it is yet.

> *"Empty space is not nothing; it is a powerful something. Learn to use it."* —Yoda

Return to Wu Chi as often as you like. Meditators try to meditate for twenty minutes twice a day. Martial artists use it to access nature's power and to attain enlightenment. If you can't find twenty minutes at a time, try two ten-minute sessions during the day. It allows you to listen innocently to nature's way or pulse without ego or objective. Thinking about it theoretically won't improve your ability in the same way thinking of playing the piano won't improve your skills without practice. It's weight lifting for the mind. Meditating not only changes how you feel during meditation but it changes your brainwaves, energy, and perception during your everyday activity.

Meditation is your way to access Wu Chi and one way to allow your qi to flow evenly through your body without blockages or deficiencies. During meditation, you become aware of your internal chatter and notice your uncontrolled thoughts (white noise) that interfere with your ability to perceive. Meditation allows us to go beyond our judgments, opinions, impressions, likes, and dislikes. There are many types of meditations. Below, I'll share three of my favourite types.

1) TM (Transcendental Meditation)

In my opinion, Transcendental Meditation is the best and easiest form of meditation. It's effortless and requires no hard concentration or focus, just easy repetition of a mantra (internal sound vibration). What I like about this form of meditation is that your thoughts are a natural part of the process, and not something you struggle against. It's effortless. Negative thoughts and emotions come and go, you don't hold on, and, gradually, you experience less of them.

I did my research before taking it up and found that Transcendental Meditation has the most scientifically proven benefits.

Meditation is a completely different state. It's the fourth state. The other three states are waking, sleeping, and dreaming. Each state has its distinctive brainwave correlation. During meditation, your brainwaves change from waking "beta" waves to "alpha" waves, and your stress hormone cortisol decreases, which leads to improved productivity and creativity.

Oprah Winfrey, Doctor Oz, *Forbes,* and the Mayo Clinic all recommend it.

> I brought Transcendental Meditation teachers into Harpo Studios to teach me and my team how to meditate. So, we started meditating. Seven of us lead to 70, led to 270, led to now everyone in the company meditates. Nine o'clock in the morning, and 4:30 in the afternoon no matter what is going on, we stop and we meditate.
> And that way of being 'still' with ourselves—coming back to the center—and recognizing that something is more important than you, it's more important than the work you are doing, brings a kind of energy and an intensity of energy, an intention that we have never had before.
> And you can't imagine what has happened in the company. People who used to have migraines, don't. People are sleeping better. People have better relationships. People interact with other people better. It's been fantastic.[9]

The following is taken from the TM website: http://www.tm.org

> *"The TM technique relies on a subtle effect of sound in bringing your mind-body system to a physiological state of deep relaxation. And as confirmed by science, this state of alert restfulness leads – through lower breathing rate, decreased stress hormone concentration and increased brain coherence – to an overall improvement in your physical and mental condition."*

Transcendental meditation has been repeatedly proven effective through hundreds of peer-reviewed studies over the years. TM has been shown to have the following benefits:

- Anti-aging. Increased telomeres
- Increased intelligence
- Greater work efficiency

- Better problem-solving and decision-making skills
- Improved leadership and management skills
- Improved relationships
- Better sleep
- Lower blood pressure
- Lower stress and better coping skills
- Decreases work stress and burnout
- Improved job satisfaction
- Balanced hormones
- Lower risk of heart disease
- Increased recovery from alcoholism
- Reduced PTSD symptoms

2) Tibetan Singing Bowl Meditation

Tibetan Singing Bowls are a relaxing way to enter Wu Chi. You can buy Tibetan Singing Bowl CDs or just go to YouTube and you'll find free sessions. Just close your eyes and listen to the sounds. Tibetan monks use singing bowls for meditation and healing. The sounds correspond to various chakras (energy centers) in the body and they entrain your vibrations to them. Just sit quietly with eyes closed and listen.

3) Meditating in and on Nature

The tai chi saying is "borrow strength from the earth." Choose a quiet, peaceful place. Old tai chi masters would choose a tree they felt had special energy and would try to practice under it whenever possible. Find a comfortable place to sit, close your eyes, and listen to nature's symphony. Be still and notice the sounds, smells, and tactile sensations (breezes, sun, etc.). Pay close attention and notice how your mind goes to a quiet place behind the sounds and sensations.

Go barefoot on the grass, sand, or dirt to "ground" yourself. It feels wonderful, works the pressure points on the sole of your feet, synchronizes your internal rhythms, and helps you become mindful of the present moment. It grounds you by allowing the Earth's negatively charged ions to enter through your feet through the "Bubbling Well" acupuncture point and allow the earth's healing qi to flow up into you. Being in the forest near a waterfall or on a beach is particularly relaxing and energizing because there are more negative ions present in natural settings. If you're in the city, find a park and sit under a tree with your shoes off.

We're naturally drawn back to nature. It reenergizes and restores us. Sunlight helps our brains produce the neurotransmitter serotonin that makes us feel good and it's converted to melatonin, which helps us sleep at night. Being surrounded by plants and trees lowers our stress hormones, blood pressure, and improves our ability to think clearly.

Dr. Mercola touts the benefits of being barefoot in his September 20, 2012 article
"Why Walking Barefoot Might Be an Essential Element of Good Health." He quotes several researchers and makes the point that:

> You are an electrical being – your body regularly produces positive charges, which can oxidize and harm you if it is excessive. The earth's surface is electrically conducive; it maintains a negative charge with its free electron supply continually replenished by global atmospheric electrical circuit.

Dr. Mercola then goes on to say:

> The scientific theory behind the health benefits seen from this simple practice is that since the Earth has a greater negative charge than your body, you end up absorbing electrons from it. This, in my understanding, is one of the most potent antioxidants we know of and may have an anti-inflammatory and antioxidant effect on your body.

Click on the following articles to learn about the benefits of being in nature.

This Is Your Brain on Nature.[10]
Nature Calms the Brain and Heals the Body[11]
How Does Nature Impact Our Wellbeing?[12]

Entering Wu Chi is restful. You'll notice that thoughts just pop into your mind without your permission or conscious intention. Just watching these thoughts will create distance between you and them and just allow you to BE. Being still and letting your mind settle down will bring you internal peace. Being still without attachment to your opinions, idea, and judgments is very freeing. When your mind quiets, your body will relax and your awareness and perception will improve.

Try a simple meditation.

Sit tall in a comfortable position in a quiet place that has no distractions for fifteen or twenty minutes. Keep a straight spine. Let your palms fall comfortably on your lap. Feel the weight of your eyelids and let them close naturally. Give yourself half a minute to observe your thoughts. Next, just think the mantra "Aum" (pronounced Ahhhh, uhhh, mmmmm) silently. Think the mantra repeatedly. Your own thoughts will come and go and that's part of the process. See your thoughts as clouds moving across the sky of your mind. Simply return your attention back to "Aum" when you notice you've been distracted. When finished, keep your eyes closed and stop thinking the mantra for a minute or two to complete the process.

Part 3 - Do Leadership Tai Chi – Flow with the Five Seasons

"The only thing that endures over time is the law of the farm. According to natural laws and principles, I must prepare the ground, put in the seed, cultivate, weed, and water if I expect to reap a harvest...there is no quick fix." —Stephen Covey

This is Part 3 in the Way. Follow the five seasons or elements in this step and put focus on your people's growth and actualization, and the rest will take care of itself. Remember that they're all related to nurturing life, health, growth, regeneration, and realization of individual expression. Don't forget that you, your people, and your customers make up your business. All of you are part of nature, and nature grows in a predictable cyclical way. The Chinese believe that there are five elements and five seasons. Each of the five elements creates one element and destroys another in the process of creation and renewal. Late Summer is the fifth season, and we'll be including it in the Way.

Nature doesn't start with providing a bountiful harvest. It grows from nothing to small (seed) to large and then disintegrates back into nothingness. Growth requires balance between stillness (yin) and activity (yang) and optimal soil and growing conditions (nurturing).

As the crops start to grow, the farmer is attentive but doesn't overdo his response in late Spring and Early Summer. It is all about balancing yin and yang. Too much or too little of anything (sun, water, nutrients, fertilizer, etc.) and the growth will suffer or cease. Aim to balance yin and yang in everything you do, feel, and express; for example, stillness and action, listening and talking, thinking and feeling.

In fall and winter, it seems as if nothing is happening, but that's far from true. Leaves fall and become compost for the next growing season. Learning, rest, reflection, and information flow is happening.

So, begin the Way in stillness and reflection, Fall or Winter. You will take the compost/learning from the previous season and create the growing conditions of the cultural soil for the next season. Think of your people as a reflection of your seeds. The important part is to expand your awareness of yourself and others and use your yi mind

The Way of Effortless Leadership

to **create a clear intention** of what you want to create or happen and then be present and flow (adjust) naturally as things change.

So, remember, wherever you are in the cycle, follow the order of the seasons with the five C's. Sometimes, you may be doing things simultaneously.

1. In Winter, **CULTIVATE SELF** (choose the seed).
2. In Spring, **CULTIVATE CULTURE** (prepare the soil or optimal growing conditions for your people).
3. During Summer **COACH AND CREATE,** (Sow the seed. Coach your people to cultivate their characters and energies; create and implement new missions, visions, structure, strategies, values, initiatives, policies, programs, etc. that support the culture; and watch it start to grow).
4. In Late Summer **CHANGE AND HARVEST RESULTS** (Flow with change and adjust. Tend and plant new crops).
5. In Fall, **CONSOLIDATE LEARNING** and reflect (plough).

Winter – Cultivate Self

"Knowing others is wisdom; knowing yourself is enlightenment."
—Lao Tzu

You've already returned to Wu Chi (the Void or the Source) in Part 2. Maintain this connection to the source as you begin cultivating your being in this next step. Self-cultivation isn't a one-time event but an ongoing process and involves the integration of body-mind-spirit. **You're the seed from which everything will grow.**

"Improve yourself into the kind of person you yourself would follow wholeheartedly and without hesitation. Learn to accept the natural progress that occurs when you act with proper principles, and seek no progress at the expense of those principles." —I Ching

Those I've coached have taught me what people want and don't want in a leader. They don't want or expect a perfect leader. The image of perfection turns off most people. People want you to be human, self-aware, humble, self-monitoring, and committed to self-development/self-cultivation. They want you to be authentic, well meaning, flexible, real, down-to-earth, sincere, humorous, imperfect, and accepting of imperfection. People will give fully of themselves to noble causes if you show that you care about them and are sincere about making a true difference.

> *"He who tries to shine*
> *Dims his own light."*
> —*Tao Te Ching* (24), Lao Tzu

Many leaders think the way to success is to harden themselves, be impressive, show no vulnerability, and lead only from their head. The Way is different and requires the whole you. **The Chinese see the mind, body, and spirit cultivation as inseparable.**

"We can think of the three treasures—jing (sexual energy), qi, shen (spirit)—as the body, mind and spirit. Some religions emphasize denying the body, or the 'flesh,' to use Saint Paul's terminology; and seeking the spirit. Qigong philosophy is the just the opposite. **It is impossible to find spirit without integrating the experience of the body**. This idea is reflected in perhaps the most famous qigong maxim: 'refine the jing to create qi; refine qi to create shen; refine shen and return to the Void (Wu Chi).' Subtle energies are based on denser ones, in the way that steam rises from boiling water.

The Way of Effortless Leadership

If you wish to develop your mind, pay attention to the body. If you wish to develop your spirit, pay attention to the mind." —
Kenneth S. Cohen, *The Way of Qigong*

The last part of Mr. Cohen's quote is key. **Pay attention to and purify the body first, and you'll develop your mind. Pay attention to and purify your mind (thoughts), and you'll develop your spirit.**

Self-cultivation requires that you ensure that you pay equal attention to the body, the mind, and the spirit. The body must be what the Chinese call **"sung"** or **relaxed and tranquil.** *Relaxation and tranquility dissolve physical and mental rigidity and allow your qi to flow naturally, improve your thinking, and raise your spirit (vibrations).* So, it's important to do mind-body exercises that improve your qi, dissolve rigidity in your thinking, and open your awareness internally and externally. By becoming sung/relaxed and tranquil, you'll be able to listen to energy or what the Chinese call to **"ting jing."** Listening to energy will allow you to be able to **"dong jing"** understand and direct the qi energy.

Vibration is the way the universe and the way nature creates change. Nothing beats a leader who's genuinely still, warm, caring, compassionate, and concerned about others. Through the self-reflection exercises in Chapter 8 and other feedback, you'll start on a path of letting go of self-limiting beliefs, concepts, prejudices, biases, mental models, opinions, ideas etc. that are making and keeping you rigid and getting in your way of being fully present, sensitive, and attentive to your people and change. You're aiming to become like an internal martial artist, soft, flexible, and responsive, needing to move only as much as necessary. It's all about self-mastery.

The Way is simple but is sometimes hard on the ego. You must be willing to hear the uncomfortable, be vulnerable, and be open to changing yourself.

A trusted boss and mentor provided me with invaluable feedback and coaching. It was a hard pill I had to swallow because it challenged what I saw as my identity. She said that I have good ideas, am client-centered, and listen well when I'm in a consultant or coach role. However, when I'm working in a different capacity as a colleague, my beliefs and behaviour sometimes change for the worse. I can get fixated on my ideas, become too intense, and lose perspective and the ability to listen and accept new information. I believe in the supremacy of the "right" idea. I've had trouble separating my being/identity from my ideas. In my mind, I'm my ideas. This is where my awareness gets blocked, my thinking gets rigid, and my energy changes. It takes me out of flow. My intention to contribute innovative ideas cannot be heard sometimes because of my force in pushing them; no one wants to have ideas pushed on them. Sometimes, your greatest strength can become your biggest weakness. I realize that part of me is insecure. I'm worried that my ideas aren't good enough and won't be heard. Ironically and unconsciously, I've sabotaged myself.

Now, I stop identifying my being with my ideas. I try to stay consciously aware and mindful of my tendency to push my ideas. I realize that being right isn't enough. I can see that if I were pitching an idea to myself, I would think, "Hey, too intense. Listen to me; you don't have the corner on good ideas." I don't like this about myself, as my behaviour is counter to my guiding principles and values of trying to bring out the best in people and have them self-cultivate and evolve. I'm committed to learning and cultivating three things: silence (be quiet), calmness (turn down the intensity) and openness (listen to learn before selling). Similarly, you should be open to discovering things you and others don't like about yourself. So, if you're feeling brave, let's begin. Turn inward.

It's difficult, if not impossible, to give your full attention to others in business if your body, mind, or spirit is unhealthy. Paying attention to your physical, emotional, and spiritual pain/well-being is the first step. So, pay close attention. Become mindful of what's happening inside your mind and body. What are your thoughts, feelings, emotions, and bodily sensations telling you? What are the stories you have about you and others that are playing in your head? Notice them without judging them. Doing this brings you into the present moment and stops you from acting unconsciously on autopilot, giving you more self-control.

1) **Review information from:**
    - Chapter 8, Your Life Lens
    - Any leadership assessments, 360 degree, and performance appraisals

The Way of Effortless Leadership

2) **Have a medical check-up** and consider your doctor's recommendations to improve your physical, mental, and emotional health.

3) **Cultivate and balance your qi** or prana (internal energy) and relax your body; this will help you self-cultivate and improve your physical, mental, emotional, and spiritual energy through:
- Taking up tai chi, yoga, and qigong. These arts have a more profound effect on your wellbeing because they're mind/body exercises that balance your energy and provide you with a relaxed sense of wellbeing. They also complement the work you did in Step One, returning to Wu Chi because qi is the source energy. In fact, tai chi is often called a moving meditation. There's stillness within the movement.
- Getting outdoors. Ideally, walk barefoot on the grass/ground. This helps give you a broader perspective and allows you to absorb the earth's negative ions that increase your chi and make you feel better.
- Getting, petting, and walking a pet. Looking into your dog's eyes will teach you how to just BE with another being without goal orientation.
- Travelling, which helps broaden your awareness, perspective, guiding principles, and values.
- Acupuncture and acupressure, which helps the flow of qi through your meridians.
- Massage therapy, which will relax your muscle tension.
- Hypnosis, which helps you dissolve unhelpful patterns and ways of thinking.
- Taking up sports and interests that require you to use nature as an ally.
- Taking time to BE with friends, family, and coworkers.
- Making friends with someone whom you would normally avoid and watch your automatic internal reactions.

4) **Observe Yourself**

Turning inward is key to understanding yourself. This season is about using self-reflection to uncover and often unlearn automatic responses, habits, compulsions, revulsions, patterns, and ways of thinking.

"To know oneself is to study oneself in action with another person." —Bruce Lee

- Be what Henry Thoreau called "the witness self." Quietly watch your own internal climate (thoughts, feelings, emotions, bodily sensations, hard held beliefs, biases, mental models, compulsions, emotions, triggers, etc.) Notice where you operate on automatic. Notice when and where your thinking and feelings get stuck and rigid. Notice when negative or extreme thoughts replay themselves. Observe where there's tension and pain in your body. Just watch them, don't try to change them. Be conscious of when and of what you're fearful. Just observe as a spectator who's detached from them.

- Cultivate a more generous spirit and positive qualities you want to generate within yourself. Scan your whole body with an internal smile, relaxing it and setting the stage. Develop the following within yourself:
    - Gratitude
    - Joy
    - Caring/compassion/love
    - An attitude of letting things be
    - Honesty
    - Stillness
    - Playfulness
    - Spontaneity
    - Patience
    - Simplicity
    - Acceptance
    - Sincerity
    - Interest. Inquiry. The beginner's mind
    - Openness, flexibility of thought/lack of prejudice
    - Light-heartedness/humour
    - Humility
    - Forgiveness

- Use Einstein's favourite "Thought Experiments" (daydreaming, imagining) to test/play out new ideas in your mind.

The Way of Effortless Leadership

- Be mindful, observe yourself before, during, and after interactions with people. Instead of being concerned with how they behave, focus on what you're thinking and feeling about them. What stories do you have about yourself and other people? What are the stories about people you dislike? Become aware of your thinking. Notice if you're prejudging. Be honest with yourself. Just notice. What do you think, feel, and expect from them. Just watch your thinking and automatic reactions. This is a way to learn more about yourself.

- What are your expectations, wants, and desires? How are these changing your BEING and behaviour?

- Observe other people's body language, sound of voice, and facial expressions, and notice how they're reacting to you. If you notice people holding back, shutting down, and not being open and expressive, you have some work to do.

- Journal. Return to your office and take some notes about what you noticed about your thinking and feeling while you were interacting with a certain person. Do the same with every person you meet. These can be quick notes.

- The idea is to access your blind spots and see opportunities for self-growth. So, you'll need to actively challenge your self-perceptions and biases.

- Choose three areas that you want to make progress in and in which you're willing to let go.

- Imagine yourself already possessing the spirit and improved abilities.

- Use your imagination to see yourself thinking, feeling, and BEING the way you want to be.

- Imagine your people noticing the change in you. Project the ideal climate where your people are inspired, trusting, loving their work, and giving their all. Just keep the picture (clear intention) in your mind and return to it often.

- Don't try too hard.

5) Uncover Your Core - Deepest Values and Vision

This next part is essential and will allow you to strip away all of the conditioning, cynicism, and resignation that **have hidden your authentic self.** Your adult critical mind will laugh at you, but just tell it to be quiet. Please take the time to do this exercise in a quiet place where you feel your best.

- Let your imagination take you back to when you were a child. What vision did you have of the ideal world in which you wanted to live? How did you want to live and act in this world? How did people treat each other? Just write down everything and anything that comes to mind. Do NOT edit. Just let the ideas flow out of you until there's nothing left. Draw, write, do whatever it takes to bring out your deepest hopes for our world.

- Now, look back at what you wrote. Circle the main themes.

- Take the themes and write a short summary of the world in which you want to live. What is your personal vision for our world? What core values do you believe will create such a world?

- This personal Vision and Values Summary will help you cultivate yourself in a way that's unique, personal, and authentic to you. Leading from this place will bring you into alignment with your deepest Self, and people will sense it.

What will happen over time is that your new conscious self-awareness and self-cultivation will change your own wavelength (vibrational frequency). This new vibe will create a climate of openness for the next Season Spring, when you'll actively cultivate cultural change.

When you make a change within yourself, people initially become leery because they wonder if it's being done with sincere, well-meaning intent and not just as a political ploy. It shakes up their sense of "reality" and what they "know" as true. So, smile and warm

The Way of Effortless Leadership

yourself inside and create sincere positive intention before starting a conversation with anyone.

It may take some time for people to trust your intentions, but stay consistent and you'll notice the difference in their reactions, trust, and engagement.

"Watch your thoughts;
They become words.
Watch your words;
They become actions.
Watch your actions;
They become habits.
Watch your habits;
They become your character.
Watch your character;
It becomes your destiny."
—Lao Tzu

"To keep the body in good health is a duty…otherwise we shall not be able to keep our mind strong and clear." —Buddha

Spring – Cultivate Culture (Prepare the Soil)

"The reason why the universe is eternal is that it does not live for itself; it gives life to others as it transforms." — Lao Tzu

It is now time to prepare the soil for growth. It is time to create a sacred culture where safety, uniqueness, diversity of thought, flow of energy, communication, and appreciation is the soil. Get rid of fear and obedience mentality. Now that you've done the hard work and started looking inward at yourself and cultivating a new way of being, it's time to put your attention on others.

"Train people well enough so they can leave. Treat them well enough so they don't want to." —Richard Branson

Neuroscience has provided us with important information on what we need to do as leaders to create a healthy, productive, and innovative culture. Neuroscientists have proven that our environment and our relationships literally shape our brain and affect how well it functions. They've also proven that the brain can and does grow and change at any age; this is called brain plasticity. Whatever you think and do repeatedly creates new neural pathways and connections, so what you think, feel, and do changes your brain. The brain's default mode of operation is that of a "threat detector," which helps us survive physical threats by triggering the fight, flight, or freeze response. When this response is triggered, the primitive part of the brain, the amygdala, draws energy from the more evolved parts of the brain. The prefrontal cortex is responsible for higher-level thinking. Unfortunately, the threat response also is triggered when we're excluded, criticized, or bullied, and it impairs our brain. The fight, flight, or freeze response impairs our productivity, working memory, analytical thinking, creative insight, and problem-solving ability. We become distracted, make more mistakes, and, if it continues for a long time, experience physical and psychological burnout. David Rock came up with the SCARF model to help leaders realize that anything they do that impacts people's sense of Status, Certainty, Autonomy, Relatedness, and Fairness may trigger the brain's stress response.

Neuroscience tells us that compassion is built into us and helps us survive and thrive. We have "Mirror Neurons," which allow us to feel empathy and self-reflect. **We need a compassionate, trusting, and peaceful culture so that our fight, flight, or freeze response isn't triggered.** When we're socially praised or validated, our brains

The Way of Effortless Leadership

are flooded with dopamine and serotonin, making us feel better, let go of worry and fixation, and be open to what other people are saying. These positive emotions and feelings synthesize neuropeptides.

Think of your own self-cultivation (inner work) that you began in the previous part/chapter and its resulting changes on your energy and behaviour as being the living expression of the world in which you want to inhabit. Your internal vibrations and behaviours act as an inspirational and aspirational model of the way you want the larger world to be and the difference you want your people and business to make. When you come from a place of complete authenticity, you become a natural and dynamic communicator because you can just be yourself, not the usual corporate talking head. Being YOU allows your passion, vision, and values to naturally emerge. Your people will want to join you on your mission because it's exciting and has heart and soul. Give them a **peaceful, harmonious, and collaborative** environment in which they can thrive and begin to cultivate themselves in the same way you're doing.

"You must be the change you want to see in the world" —Mahatma Gandhi

Many leaders put a lot of attention on the customer experience, but the employee experience (the culture) must come first. When your people feel important, trusted, and appreciated by you, they'll love coming to work and serve their customers with loving attention. Thus, the customer experience will take care of itself. They won't shy away from telling you the truth for fear that you'll use it against them. Use your compassion, love, stillness, and positive intent to do right by your people by creating a warm and hospitable climate to help them go beyond business-centered learning and help them self-cultivate, self-realize, and evolve. The Vancouver-based company Lululemon tasks their managers with the responsibility and privilege of coaching their people to reach personal as well as business goals, even to the point of them choosing to leave for a competitor.

"I offer you peace. I offer you love. I offer you friendship. I see your beauty. I hear your need. I feel your feelings. My wisdom flows from the Highest Source. I salute that Source in you. Let us work together for unity and love." —Mahatma Gandhi

Maintain a positive and optimistic attitude. Get to know all of your people and their highest aspirations. Make everything about them.

Communicate your deepest core values and highest aspirations, inquire about theirs, and then build a vision or noble cause of common values that impassions your team. Your vibrations will be felt and will lead to peace, productivity, and empowerment. Be trusting, don't push (it only creates resistance), and give people space. If you do so, you won't have to force alignment; people will just want to be a cocreator in the world you're giving them and will want to share it with others.

"Just as some diseases are contagious, we've found that many emotions can pulse through social networks."

"Happiness isn't one big event, but the accrual of smaller, incremental steps, such as feeling gratitude and helping others."

"Rather than asking how we can get happier, we should be asking how we can increase happiness all around us. When you make positive changes in your own life, those effects ripple out from you and you can find yourself surrounded by the very thing you fostered." —Harvard Medical School professor of medical sociology and medicine Nicholas Christakis

Look at how fast children grow, learn, and create. What do they do differently from adults? They self-express, move, play, experiment, have fun, share, and don't give up when they fail. Contrast that to most of our workplaces. Notice the difference. It's a fact that we innovate during times of rest/distraction/play.

Recently, I attended a Human Resources Conference in Vancouver, BC on Power, and I was impressed with many of the keynote speakers. I was struck by the number of speakers who put a focus on the importance for leaders to differentiate the employee experience and shift corporate culture from being competitive to collaborative, to one in which everyone is treated as important. They focused on what it really takes to engage the hearts and minds of people. Themes revolved around believing in people's ability; showing empathy; listening; emotional well-being; engaging the heart and mind; and creating a safe space where everyone has freedom, is important to the team, and has a voice. Counsellors and coaches have known the value of these aspects for many years, and it was nice to see them going mainstream. However, the biggest problem from my conversations with multiple HR professionals at roundtables and conferences is that they feel that senior leadership is solely focused on business results and financial matters and see anything that resembles "warm and fuzzy" as irrelevant.

Sean Fitzpatrick's session on "Employee Engagement to Employee Experience" proved that what leaders have been doing has NOT worked to engage their people. Sean works for Telemap and conducts Engagement Surveys. He shared that North American companies spend $1.5 Billion to study employee engagement annually, yet, over many years, engagement has remained flat with no improvement.

Margaret Heffernan, in her keynote address, "The One Firm Firm: How to Get the Best from Everyone," spoke about the importance of creating a culture where "everyone matters." She highlighted the BP accident at Deep Water Horizon where many people died because of an internal culture that encouraged organizational silence. She pointed out that recent studies have shown that "85% of people said they don't voice their concerns at work." She also said that "we would rather be wrong than alone" and "that most people are obedient conformists." She spoke about how the airline industry turned around a poor safety record in the 1970s by creating a "just culture" where "people could say what was on their minds." She believes that cultures should provide more freedom and feedback and hire for generosity, reciprocity, trust, and curiosity - not grades. Margaret said, "We can't afford high potential programs, as they say to others 'you have no potential.'" She mentioned that it has been proven that top teams have three things in common: empathy, equal contribution from every member, and more women. The "mortar (energy and relationships) is more important than the bricks."

Another keynote speaker at the conference was Josh Bershen. His talk was "The Future of Work: Ways HR Should Adapt." He said that in this world of digital disruption, the jobs of the future "are more human" and people are seeking cultures where emotional well-being and their whole life can be nurtured. It's incumbent upon leaders to "design and differentiate the employee experience." They want a place where "they can be themselves at work." He also said, "Performance appraisals actually reduce performance." Leaders must have continuous conversations with their people and have fewer goals to be effective, engage their people, and improve performance.

The Mental Health Commission of Canada commissioned a National Standard of Canada - Psychological Health and Safety in the Workplace_paper. It was published in January 2013 by the CSA and BNQ. The document speaks to five key areas that both law and science agree leaders need to take seriously in cultivating a healthy workplace culture.

1. Ensure job demands don't exceed skill level.
2. Allow people to have job control and self-express.
3. Be fair.
4. Praise.
5. Support them.

Let me share three stories.

The first is one I consider a failure on my part. However, it provided me with insight many years later. I first went into one organization as a consultant and had a confidential conversation with the top dog. I won't use her real name. Let's call her Dawn. Dawn thought her staff was completely incompetent and said to me, "None of my staff can think for themselves" and "If I had my druthers, I'd fire every one of my staff." At the end of the conversation, Dawn wanted to hire coaches to "fix her people." I felt something wasn't quite right, given her comments, but she was the client. I agreed to source the coaches for her people but also suggested she use one as well. This woman did have a dysfunctional staff. There was a lot of infighting and a complete lack of innovation or engagement. There was no energy, creativity, passion, or collaboration; however, as I got to witness Dawn's way of operating, it soon became clear that she had created the problem. Dawn treated her superiors with respect and her subordinates with disdain. She micro-managed and would talk behind people's backs, bringing them down in the eyes of others. She would blame her mistakes on her people and take the credit for others' accomplishments, further eroding her people's confidence in themselves and others. There was stagnation and no innovation. People kept their heads low and their minds on their own self-protection and job security. Dawn's people lived down to her expectations. Dawn was oblivious and unwilling to see how her own lack of awareness, disharmonious and destructive perception, energy, and behaviour impacted the entire culture. She saw all her people problems as being generated externally.

The second story is about one of the best bosses I've had in my life. Richard always seemed at peace with himself and never hurried. When he interviewed me, he set the stage for our relationship. He asked me what my mission was and I gave him a business card on which was written, "Inspiring self-expressed lives." He said with a glint in his eye, "I love it! However, your tie is crooked." Slightly

The Way of Effortless Leadership

embarrassed, I laughed and admitted that I was "the no-tie guy" and wore it out of respect for his corporate culture. Richard said, "You can be yourself here. Lose the tie." He would walk around throughout the day with a smile on his face and join in conversations, observing the energy and interaction around him. Richard would often bring us into his office to discuss our personal and professional goals. He was genuinely interested and he would ask, "So, how are things going?" "What do you need?" and "How can I help?" He got out of our way and we rose to the occasion. You could feel his calm and compassionate energy before he said anything. He would also give public credit to his people for the successes and he would always stand in front of us and take the responsibility, taking the fire when things went askew. Everyone loved working for Richard. We all felt trusted and capable in his eyes and secure in our positions. The office energy and the engagement were very high. We all collaborated and innovated together, and we felt a sense of common purpose. Richard knew that his way of being and his behaviour was a model for the rest of us to follow.

The third story is about my father. My dad, who was a senior executive at a large insurance company well before the corporate disruption (downsizing, restructuring) in the 1980s, inspired my philosophy. His people loved working for him and were fully engaged as he created a wonderful corporate culture that was all about their growth and achieving mutual goals. He was still and calm. He said the company had an obligation to be loyal to its people, something unheard of today. He believed his job was to help people grow and develop and to remove those things that impeded them from doing so. He mentored people, gave them credit, enriched people's jobs by making them more interesting, gave them more authority where they could sign off on large payout cheques (up to a million dollars) without need for his approval, simplified processes, eliminated red tape, and had one rule with people: that he would not tolerate negative, harmful gossip about others.

In relation to learning, we require time to process external change. We can learn new habits at any age, but learn best through self-discovery, but only when we're mindful of what we're doing. Mindfulness requires **a safe and peaceful environment where we can concentrate**. Consider making this your aim for your culture.

Set a clear intention in your mind of the culture you want to create. Begin cultivating an environment that will bring out the best in your people by:

1. Making it a culture where everyone matters.
2. Creating a climate where organizational silence is rooted out. Model brave expressive truth telling. Encourage, recognize, and reward people to self-express, challenge status-quo thinking, bring concerns, have difficult conversations, and suggest new ideas.
3. Being mindful of your internal thoughts, opinions, and prejudices.
4. Accepting yourself (faults and all) fully.
5. Creating a safe, sacred, peaceful space that encourages expression.
6. Making the culture nurture life, learning, growth, self-awareness, exploration, appreciation, communication (amongst all teams and levels), and truth telling.
7. Getting rid of internal silos and competition (us against them mentality). Model and highlight the value in inter- and intra-team collaboration.
8. Sharing your deeply held vision and values.
9. **Seeing others as whole and complete, lacking nothing**. See them as having everything they need to blossom and perform.
10. Making your people your top priority. Focusing on the growth and development of your people. Help each person be "**Zi ran**" or true to themselves and their path.
11. Being still, the calm in the middle of the storm.
12. Being real and letting go.
13. Not pretending to have all the answers. Show your humanity and vulnerability.
14. Truth telling. Don't punish it. Reward it in others.
15. Hiring and promoting people with diverse perspectives.
16. Being compassionate and recognizing and rewarding this quality in others.
17. Not hiring and promoting yes men and women intent on self-promotion.
18. Promoting people with who are natural listeners and who enjoy coaching and developing others. Hard skills are easy to teach, soft people skills almost impossible.
19. Taking more of the blame when things go wrong and giving others credit when things go right.
20. Setting a clear intention to create a culture that aligns with human nature.
21. Trusting and providing people with autonomy.
22. Providing them with support and resources.

The Way of Effortless Leadership

23. Praising and rewarding people. Appreciation fuels motivation.
24. Listening to your people with the intention to learn and appreciate.
25. Encouraging your staff to voice their opinions.
26. Coaching and asking questions that has them observe their thinking.
27. Self-monitoring. Be aware of your face and body language. Smile. Open your body.
28. Encouraging those who challenge the status quo because they're courageous enough to not kiss ass and are trying to make a difference.
29. Providing space for distraction, downtime, and reflection. This will reduce stress and increase innovation.
30. Encouraging movement. Physical movement oxygenates your brain.
31. Telling stories. People remember stories easily.
32. Providing challenge that's just above people's skill level. Too little and they'll get bored. Too much and they'll stress out.
33. Creating a sense of play and fun.
34. Allowing even encouraging well-meaning failure. It fuels innovation.
35. Designing a work space that follows good design principles that encourages people to move easily throughout the workplace, encouraging cross-functional communication and optimal health.
36. Meditating together. Have 10-minute group meditations with your team, followed by a gratitude sharing before beginning your day or meeting.
37. Being completely present with someone without judgment or agenda.
38. Encouraging people to take breaks in nature. Nature has an abundance of qi and negative ions that make one feel good and relax.
39. Encouraging other leaders to join you in creating a welcoming culture.
40. Shaking hands. Touch builds energetic connection and trust.
41. Allowing yourself to be spontaneous with people.
42. Asking questions that show you care and want to build it together.

43. Not being afraid of people with "fringe" ideas. Innovation usually comes from these people, so welcome them into the fold.
44. Protecting the safe space you've created. Make it clear that harmful gossip and bullying won't be tolerated. Let go or weed out poisonous people who gossip, seek to damage the culture, and bully or harm others. Only do this as a last resort.
45. Consider making your organization dog friendly. Dogs in a workplace allow people to experience nature in the office and they make them more relaxed, softer, and more compassionate to each other. I brought my dog to work and noticed the transformations in people's energy.
46. Laughing frequently. It eases tension.
47. Taking no credit for any successes. Give the credit to your people.
48. Having Stay Interviews. Ask your people what they love about the place and makes them want to stay. Ask them what sort of things might make them want to leave.
49. Starting a company vegetable garden. This will allow employees to have first-hand experience in growing something together and using nature's way. It builds team spirit and grounds people in reality. Consider, having them donate some of the produce to a local food bank and have them share the remainder.

"The nature Tao teaches one to retreat after one's success and not to hold onto the credit." – *Tao Te Ching* (9), Lao Tzu

You can't force people to be productive or innovative. You can only provide a physical and cultural climate/environment that enables their natural creativity to emerge. Providing people with freedom and inspiring surroundings where they can rest their overactive mind allows the brain time to unconsciously associate ideas, make new connections, and produce new creative breakthroughs.

Well-designed buildings with play and relaxation rooms allow people to decompress, socialize, and take their minds off work. Neuroscience tells us we need this because our brains are social organs that don't work well in isolation (consider the effects of solitary confinement as a brutal punishment in the penal system). Our brains are constantly striving to make new connections and patterns, so providing opportunities for cross-functional conversations and learning works.

The Way of Effortless Leadership

Brian Borzykowski, in a May 17, 2017 article on BBC.com, wrote about
Jerry Tate, an architect and partner with London firm Tate, Harmer, and Natalie Jeremijenko, who "created TREExOffice, an enclosed outdoor office space built around a tree in London Hoxton Square…There's plenty of research to suggest that being surrounded by nature, whether that's having a view of trees and grass from an office window or having a plant at your desk, can help people work harder. A Human Spaces Global Report found that workplaces that incorporate natural elements, like greenery and sunlight, are 6% more productive and 15% more creative than offices that don't.

If that's the case, then shouldn't working outdoors should [sic] be as good, if not better, than looking out the window? 'Quite a few studies show that people become more relaxed, their heart rate slows and they become more creative when they connect with an outdoor natural environment,' says Tate."

In June of 2017, Global News Vancouver television station reported that CBRE Group Inc.'s Vancouver office became the first workplace to receive the prestigious WELL Certification gold level award by the International WELL Building Institute for actively promoting employee health and wellness. There are many wellness features including providing all employees with access to natural light, inspiring views, ergonomic sit/stand desks, trees throughout the building, new technology that reduces stress-inducing noise and a culture that promotes physical movement. This work environment that promotes employee wellness is benefiting the company by allowing them to differentiate themselves as an employer of choice, enabling them to recruit and retain the best and the brightest.

Recognize and reward people who demonstrate those qualities you've cultivated within yourself and are modelling.

"Clients do not come first. Employees come first. If you take care of your employees, they will take care of your clients." —Richard Branson

"He who does not trust enough, will not be trusted" —Lao Tzu

"When 'I' is replaced by 'we' even illness becomes wellness"
—Malcolm X

The Way of Effortless Leadership

Early Summer – Create and Coach (Plant the Seed and Tend)

You're the professional and know your organization best, so we won't be going into depth about what specific things you can create, as the Way is about the "how." However, I'll provide you with a few ideas from a coach's perspective that work to engage people.

Now it's time to do two things: Create and Coach:

1. **Create and implement initiatives and solutions** that define and nurture the culture's growth.
    - It's important to think holistically and strategically, and to design **simple, common sense solutions** that align with and support the culture you started modelling in Spring. Start slowly and do NOT overwhelm people.
    - Align any new mission, vision, values, structure, strategies, business goals, programs, policies, and practices with the new spirit, natural, reality-driven values that supports life, growth, evolution, sustainability, efficiency, and wellness.
    - Choose inclusive values and goals that are based on love and deep respect and that help humanity, not just in service to specific groups.
    - Choose one or two things at a time that you think will have the best chance to succeed and have the most leverage and impact. The worst thing you can do is to create a huge number of initiatives and receive no buy-in.
    - Have retreats that are off-site and allow people to contribute their ideas in developing the strategy, values, and big goals. People support and take ownership of what they create, just as someone who owns a home usually takes more pride and care than someone who's renting a home.
    - Encourage communication & collaboration amongst people/departments by highlighting their importance and tying performance and promotional opportunities to these competencies. Continue to model them yourself.

- Promote leaders based on their character, sense of awareness, listening skills, compassion, and sincere desire to develop others. Remember, soft overcomes hard.
- Don't promote based on ego and technical skill. Leadership is a different skill. People don't want to be impressed by the leader, they want the leader to trust them, support them, and be impressed by them. Pick compassionate people who want to help others succeed.
- Redesign the physical space to allow energy, information, and ideas to flow freely.
- Consider doing as the French have done, creating a policy or practice that encourages employees to disconnect from the office by not requiring them to check email from home.
- Every day, acknowledge and validate someone on your team.

2. **Demonstrate your deep love and respect for your people/Atmans** by coaching them. Remember, great coaching starts with the quality of your being, how you hold the person in your mind, and your interest and commitment to the person's well-being and growth. If you view the person as less than, deficient, or a problem to be fixed, they'll feel it and won't trust you or the process. Coaching isn't repairing; it's transformational. You notice and encourage the individual's greatness to emerge. Great coaching isn't about applying techniques; it's about relationship, trust, and mutual engagement. Remember, you're aiming not to try hard but to use effortless action or Wu Wei.

- Have weekly one-on-one meetings with each of your people (thirty minutes max).
- Build rapport quickly and trust over time. Without these, the coaching relationship won't work.
- Coach and facilitate your people's growth and evolution. Show sincere and deep interest in each person and help them to become Zi Ran or Self-so.

The Way of Effortless Leadership

- Give the person your full and undivided attention by maintaining eye contact and listening with the intent to understand, feel, and learn. This demonstrates your deep respect for their internal Atman.
- Have conversations designed around helping them observe and improve their thinking.
- Look to "catch" what they're doing well, what's working well, and bring it to their attention.
- Continue to smile, internally and externally. Maintain a positive intention in your mind and envision what you want to occur.
- Encourage self-awareness.
- Allow them to share their feelings. Don't try to negate or rush them through processing. This will help you build trust.
- Allow them to set their own goals and have them write them down (have them be specific and, if possible, include timelines). If they're missing something, ask them if you can suggest one or two things.
- Don't give them the answers. Ask good open-ended questions and get them to think about how they could do things differently. If they come up with the answer, they'll own the changes, get more energy, and become even more engaged.
- Reflect on what they share.
- At times, paraphrase back to them what they've said. Doing so will make them feel valued and heard.
- Give immediate well-intentioned feedback to help them grow.
- Be willing to have the difficult conversations. It demonstrates respect. Make certain to do these in private with the door closed, and keep these conversations completely private.
- Use appropriate humour, touch (handshake).
- Ask for and use their ideas and always give them public credit.
- Let them know that you'll follow up with them on their plans. Keeping them accountable will help them reach their goals.

- Use Wu Wei (effortless effort). Flow with the conversation. Improvise; don't seek to control. Talk less but stay fully aware and engaged.
- Remember, you're not aiming to achieve a quick fix; you're nurturing the individual's self-awareness and growth. Mastery takes time, so be patient.

Just before I sent my manuscript off to my editor, I came across this unique and wonderful book, *Take the Reins! 7 Secrets to Inspiring Leadership* by Shari Jaeger Goodwin, business strategist, leadership coach, speaker, and trainer. She created a new leadership model Alpha Horse Leadership Training for Humans. She recounts how her resistant horse Dixie taught her how to use and shift her energy and whole being to lead effectively. She says that she uses horses in coaching leaders because they can help you in three ways: "1) The horse is a master at reading intention, 2) the horse is concerned only with the present moment—the now, and 3) the horse validates congruence—the energetic state where what you think, feel, say and do, align."

She ended up developing a strong bond with Dixie and won jumping competitions. She learned to become more self-aware of her thoughts, feelings, energy, the timing and intensity of her requests, intention, commitment, and her breath. She wrote that this new approach was

> centered on empathy—the capacity to experience the emotions of another—and my own self-awareness changed everything. This was the turning point in my horsemanship and had huge influences on my professional life outside horses. It wasn't all about me, how I felt, what I wanted, what I knew, or even what someone told me to do. For best results, I needed to truly understand what "the other" desired and needed.

Shari learned the secrets of shifting her own energy, intention, and body language to **create a vibration of neutrality and possibility**. She characterizes the energy as **safe, open, confident, nonthreatening**, and she mentions the importance of maintaining a relaxed body, steady deep breathing, and soft curious eyes. Please pick up or download her book, it's filled with wonderful stories of leaders she has coached using her horses as feedback tools.

The Way of Effortless Leadership

Shari refers to Robert Cooper's book *The Other 90%,* where he agrees with the Chinese that the three major nerve centers in your body are your "head(brain), your heart, and your gut." She stresses the importance of using your "entire being – your body and mind working together in awareness." To use the "Other 90%," you need to align your intention (visualization of the outcome), beliefs, action, and be open to adjusting your approach, given what each of the nerve centers tell you.

Shifting your internal vibrations to a neutral (open, nonfearful, nonaggressive, nongrasping) vibration is key to developing a relaxation of deep trust with your people. As you've seen, you can also use it when you go horseback riding or in dealing with your pet at home.

To improve your coaching skills, I also highly recommend you visit the International Coach Federation and check out their core competencies and training programs.[13]

I also recommend you give the following books a read. Marshall J. Cook and Laura Poole's, *Effective Coaching* – Second Edition, McGraw Hill, 2011. Gervase Bush's, *Clear Leadership,* Davies-Black Publishing, 2001. Bush teaches you about how you can cut through "interpersonal mush" with learning conversations.

Late Summer – Change and Harvest (Reap)

All of your hard work in Spring and Summer is paying off. It's harvest time. You're having or reaping results from sowing the right seeds/creating the right climate/culture in Spring. The positive cultural vibrations give people confidence, keeps communication open, and makes them more receptive and resilient to change.

This is when change usually hits. You realize you need to overhaul or tweak some things to improve your results.

People don't resist self-created change. They resist others forcing them to change. The more that you can engage people, use and acknowledge their ideas, keep them in the loop, and treat them like partners in the process, the more they'll work with you to achieve the change.

Tai chi practitioners do a two-person exercise called push hands. Partners use each other to understand how to ground/root themselves to the earth and maintain their dynamic stability (Zhong Din) in face of force and change. See change and conflict the same way. Adopt an appreciative, grateful attitude and realize you'll be helping each other grow and improve your character/skill.

I went into an organization for several months as a consultant. The company was going to be closing its operation and moving to another country in six months. I wasn't the original consultant and was thrown in at the last moment. My first day onsite was an eye-opener. I met very briefly with senior leadership prior to their announcement of the change. They shared with me that they had wonderful staff that had worked for the company, some for up to thirty-five years. It was a collaborative environment in which people and departments worked well together. Leaders were relaxed and demonstrated being in flow and using Wu Wei.

We then went into the meeting. Senior leadership met very briefly with staff in a meeting, announced that they would be shutting down operations and that I was there to help them manage change and to help their people decide if they wanted to follow the company or move on. Management had not prepared their people for the change; they left the room quickly after the announcement and left no time for questions. This was a crucial and defining moment of how the change was about to play out. Leadership had not created a well-thought-out change-management plan and had not chosen the change management sponsors/team well. The leaders had switched from being in flow and using Wu Wei (being thoughtful, relaxed, aware, transparent, communicative, informal) to using force (losing awareness, trying to control and contain the information, being stilted, fearful, formal, and ill-at-ease with themselves). I looked around the room at people's faces and could tell this wasn't going to be pretty. Sure enough, a week or two into the change, there were incidents of major vandalism, fights on the floor, a few key people quit and others were calling in sick regularly. Morale, productivity, health, and collaboration all declined. I asked those I was coaching why they thought this was happening. They said that they felt disrespected by the leaders they had trusted. They had not been allowed to ask questions, deal with their emotions, or be part of making the change happen. People felt they had been treated like disposable things as opposed to valuable, trusted unique beings/colleagues. They hadn't been kept in the loop with what was happening business-wise ahead of time. They were being overworked because people were quitting and calling in sick. They had been given six months working notice with no incentive to stay the course. Their managers weren't spending time with them and were hiding behind closed doors and not communicating. In short, they had lost complete faith and trust in their leaders. I asked people for their permission to take their comments back to leadership without names attached.

To the leaders' credit, they listened well and were shocked that they had, overnight, changed the culture and disrupted the trust that had been earned over many years. They said they themselves had been feeling very stressed with the pressure from corporate and were feeling overwhelmed with all they had to accomplish. They didn't mean to disrespect their people. They asked me what could be done. I suggested they:

- Meet with everyone as a group, be very real and vulnerable, share how the change was making them feel, and apologize for how they had been acting.
- Offer some financial incentive to those who stayed the course.
- Meet with each of their people and just let them vent.
- Listen to their concerns and ideas and keep the communication flowing.

The vandalism stopped, relationships slowly got back to normal, and trust was reestablished.

The leaders let go of the need to overcontrol, reestablished their relationship with nature, and assumed a state of information flow. I came to understand that at the time that the leaders most needed to stay in a state of flow with nature, they distrusted their own ability to stay in the present moment, and resorted to a forced approach.

The good news is that if you've been sincerely diligent and have created a positive, open, fun, and friendly environment last season, you'll find that you've built a true foundation of trust. People understand that things are changing. They'll appreciate your sincerity, compassion, and caring during this time. They'll cherish your ability to stay real and keep communication open. The stillness and patience that you cultivated within yourself will trickle throughout the organization or the team.

Most managers get stressed during change and put all their attention into the DOING of tasks, but this does NOT work. During times of great change, it's even more important to:

- Be patient. Realize that acceptance of change doesn't happen quickly. Let nature's process take its course. The paradox is that by showing real patience, your people will buy into the change more quickly.
- Share business intelligence well ahead of time so your people won't be caught off guard when change occurs and they'll understand the context.
- Just be with and listen to your people.
- Let people have their strong emotions and vent. Don't expect instant buy-in.
- Don't rush into requiring people to be task-oriented; let them digest the planned changes.
- Be still.
- Be real and sincere.
- Be more kind, compassionate, and understanding.
- Focus more on nurturing the trust in relationships.
- Respect people by planning well ahead of time.
- Be straightforward.
- Communicate early, often, and in different ways.
- See your people as partners in grappling with change, and ask and use their ideas.
- When successes happen, give all the credit to your people.

The Way of Effortless Leadership

- Implement the least number of changes possible to accomplish your goal.
- Weed carefully. Let go of those who are harmful to the spirit of safety and goodwill. One malicious person can poison the entire culture. If you have to let them go, do it early and with compassion.
- **Use Wu Wei, effortless action to flow with change.**

Fall - Consolidate Learning (Plough and Compost)

You've flowed well with change. You've kept your spirit strong and your people close. Results have improved over late Summer and early Fall. It's now time to plough the ground and allow the dead leaves to create compost for next year.

In this season, you'll assess data, review feedback, rest, conserve, store, reflect, and collect or consolidate learning/lessons for Winter.

Take the feedback from your people (conversation and 360 evaluations on you), customers, stakeholders, etc. during the previous two seasons and sit down in quiet to look at where you need to self-cultivate in Winter. Redo the "Your Life Lens" exercises in Chapter 8 and notice how your perception has changed and where you still need to do work.

You've completed one natural growth cycle. Cycles are continuous, and so will be your improvement and self-mastery. Your people will experience a real and tangible difference in you.

You'll sense a growing openness and trust that will continue to spread throughout departments and the whole organization.

Encourage other leaders to use the Way, as the more leaders who do, the greater the organizational shift.

Customers will feel the difference because your people will be genuinely much happier.

It will be easier to recruit and retain people because word will spread fast that your organization is different, not just intent upon looking good in Mission, Vision, and Values declarations and Annual Reports.

Continue using Wu Wei. Wu Wei is the key principle of nature. This will ensure that your ego doesn't get the best of you and that you're using a gentle facilitation process that puts your people ahead of anything else. You're now a Servant Leader Extraordinaire.

The Way of Effortless Leadership
Chapter 10 – Natasha's Story

> "**The way we see the problem is the problem.**" —Stephen R. Covey

This story will shed some light on what a leader can do that works, what doesn't work, and how the Way can improve the chances that things will go smoothly. It's not prescriptive and your experience will be different, but it's instructive.

Natasha is someone within my circle of contacts. She read the draft of this book and asked for some coaching in the Way in relation to one of her past work experiences. The following is based on a true story but I've changed a few details and used fictitious names.

I'll start by sharing Natasha's story. This will be followed by our coaching conversations and what she learnt about herself from applying the Way to her experience.

Natasha's Story

Natasha is a dynamic, busy, and action-oriented woman. She's a whirlwind of nonstop activity. She was a top sales person for many years. A few years back, she packed up and left America for Europe. She landed a good job as a publisher for a prominent magazine before she was thirty. This was Natasha's first position as a leader. She managed offices in several European cities and had multiple reports in each office. Natasha recounted to me that within her first few weeks on the job, she realized that none of the staff had liked her predecessor because she overwhelmed her people with new initiatives and "lorded over everyone" like a queen and "treated them like serfs." Natasha wanted to do better and be an inspiring leader. Natasha's bosses and clients had described her as a professional, objective, and critical thinker who possessed a good sense of humour. She was confident that her subjective matter expertise would ensure her success as a manager. Natasha's boss was on another continent and not readily available because of the time difference, so she didn't really have anyone with whom to discuss issues on a regular basis.

Natasha started out wanting to make a positive impact. She began looking outward, at what needed to be done to improve sales. She was task- and initiative-focused and had a project management mentality. She was smart to think about the existing negative culture and that it needed tweaking, so she implemented a Christmas bonus, summer hours, and fun staff recognition outings like disco bowling. She implemented new sales tools and shorter and more frequent sales meetings. People were pleased with the new perks, and the sales improved.

Natasha hired another mid-level sales manager. I'll call her Debbie. Natasha liked Debbie and appreciated her "quirky" and "natural" style and felt she would be an engaging and natural relationship builder with clients.

Six months into the new job, Natasha felt a lot of stress because the economy took a nosedive and customers were wary of spending on advertising. So, she doubled down and became even more detail-oriented and task-focused, overseeing everything that was happening around her. She required people to compile daily sales reports to monitor their productivity and to be able to provide them with suggestions. She became frustrated at the situation in general. She worked harder and longer hours. Her signature sense of humour waned, and she became short with people in conversation. She started closing her door to "get more work done." Around this time, Natasha noticed that people around the office seemed to be less communicative with each other. She decided that they needed more information about how to communicate with their clients, manage their workload, and close sales, so she began trying to teach them what had worked for her. She was directive and taught them her way of how to be successful. To her surprise, they didn't appreciate it the way that she had hoped.

Natasha became particularly frustrated with Debbie because she felt she wasn't as professional as she should be. She was "overly familiar" with clients and disorganized. She also seemed despondent at times. Sometimes, she would sleep in the office after going out with friends at night. Clients and staff hadn't complained about Debbie and she was performing at average level. Natasha would often lose her patience with Debbie. Natasha started micromanaging Debbie, watching and correcting everything she did. Debbie became more distant. Natasha began to see her as "having a sad life" and that she was "insecure and lonely" and thought she was "trying to gain a

The Way of Effortless Leadership

social life at work." This flew in the face of Natasha's belief that work and personal life should be kept separate.

Natasha upped her micromanaging of Debbie and developed a disdain for her. Debbie ended up hating Natasha and talking behind her back to other colleagues. Debbie's performance worsened. Other midlevel managers and staff also lost their energy, and everyone's engagement and performance decreased. Eventually, Natasha decided to leave the position of publisher and work for the same organization as a consultant. The new owners who took over fired Debbie.

"If I really want to improve the situation, I can work on one thing over which I have control – myself." —Stephen R. Covey, *The 7 Habits of Highly Effective People*

How Would You Use the Way's Principles to Coach Natasha?

What would you want to tell her? Think about what you've learnt about the Way. What did she do well? What could she have done better using the principles in this book?

My Initial Conversation with Natasha

We sat down and I asked Natasha to tell me her story and to then summarize what she thought worked and what didn't.
In terms of positives, she

1. Brought lots of initial energy, positive intention, and commitment to the success of the magazine.
2. Implemented summer hours so people had more flexibility for work/life balance and to try to improve employee commitment/engagement.
3. Implemented more social events after work to try to elevate the office spirit.
4. Used her subject matter expertise to try to help people succeed.
5. Spent one-on-one time with each person teaching them what she knew worked.
6. Was clear on her expectations.
7. Didn't want to harm Debbie, so she let her keep her job.

In terms of negatives, she said:
1. All my busyness blocked my ability to be aware and present.
2. I didn't really see or appreciate my people and treated them as things for me to accomplish my tasks to achieve goals.
3. My focus right from the start was all on DOING instead of BEING with my people and building relationships.
4. I had no stillness within myself. I was tense, anxious, and impatient.
5. I didn't understand my own developmental needs, and these negatively impacted my communication.
6. I wasn't clear with Debbie because I didn't respect Debbie's ability to learn, grow, and change and instead ignored behaviour I felt was harmful to her reputation, career, our magazine, and our culture. By choosing to brush the uncomfortable under the carpet, I damaged my relationship with her and others and, over time, lost the trust of my people.
7. I didn't have trust and confidence in my people's ability to be able to think, create, and solve.
8. My own internal vibrations were discordant and edgy and this became the culture.
9. When hard times hit and change started happening, I put more focus on DOING when I should have slowed down and demonstrated how to be aware, calm, and centered.
10. I demonstrated my distrust in people's ability by micromanaging them.
11. I taught my people like an elementary school teacher, impatiently scolding them like children.
12. In the end, there was no joy, engagement, or sense of "flow."

I then took Natasha through the "model" of the Way.

Part 1. Use Wu Wei – Effortless Effort or Forceless Action

Natasha struggled to grasp this part of the Way because she's a woman of action. This principle of nature, that to be effective, you do the absolute minimum to achieve the effect you want, was hard for Natasha because she was used to putting in hard concentration and effort, and managing her people was the sign of a dedicated and productive leader. I told her that the Way would help her improve this area in which she wanted to improve because it would require

The Way of Effortless Leadership

her to be more aware and attentive. My counsel to her was to BE more and DO less because it would demonstrate her trust in her people to think for themselves. Stepping back would allow her people to step forward.

Part 2. Wu Chi – Tap into Source

In keeping with the Flow of the Way, I taught Natasha how to meditate and how to tap into Source or the Tao/Wu Chi. I had her write down on a piece of paper what she felt and thought about it and said we'd discuss her experience at the end of the session.

Part 3. Leadership Tai Chi (Flow with The Five Seasons/Elements)

I took Natasha through the Five Seasons, starting with the first season, **Winter or Self-Cultivation,** by using Chapter 8's "Your Life Lens" exercises.

I had Natasha complete the **"My Life Balance Wheel"** exercise. She had high scores on the areas: self-image; career; finance; social and family. The areas in which she felt she needed to work on were love, rest/recreation, contribution, and personal growth and spirituality. I asked her what she noticed. She said her life wasn't balanced at the time. Outward success and recognition (yang) were highlights in her life but she had a yearning in her for more internal meaning, connection, and purpose (yin).

At the end of this session, I asked her to complete the remaining exercises in Chapter 8, "Your Life Lens" and that the information would be used in our conversation.

My Second Conversation with Natasha

A lot came out of this conversation. Natasha had completed all her homework from Chapter 8 "Your Life Lens" and when we sat down, I could tell that a light bulb had gone on.

Natasha said that the "Leadership Vision/Dreams/Hopes vs. Leadership Reality" exercise made her realize just how sad she felt about the experience. She had had all these lofty expectations of what it would be like to be a leader, and she envisioned all of her people being empowered and productive and the company succeeding, just as she had done in sales. She thought she would feel a relaxed "I've made it" feeling and was "going to have fun" when, in reality, she went home at night cynical and resigned and longing for the days she could just be on her own and not be responsible for others. She really disliked leading because she felt the position changed her and required her to be "unnatural."

Natasha spoke about the "Best vs. Worst Bosses I've Had" exercise and how she compared to them. She said, "I realized that I wouldn't like working for me. I wasn't a very good boss." The "Sentence Stem" exercise revealed that she thought "people are inherently unmotivated and lazy" and that this made her want to drive her people. In an interesting and paradoxical twist, she said she struggled with her own motivation.

In completing the exercises, Natasha realized that the bosses that had inspired her had been very different from the way she was being with her people. I asked her to choose the most important things that she wanted to start cultivating. She chose:

1. To be more curious and let go of the idea that her way is the only way to accomplish a goal.
2. To be more compassionate and less judgmental.
3. To be still, talk less and be a more effective listener/observer to subtleties.
4. To be more gentle so that she didn't come across as a "bulldozer."
5. To challenge her own laziness and lack of motivation.
6. To be more patient.
7. To be conscious, to open her awareness to things and other people's energy and behaviour that she would normally ignore.
8. To stop procrastinating difficult conversations.

At the end of this session, we reviewed her recent experience with meditation. She noticed how uncontrolled, automatic, and busy her thoughts were and how, at first, they interfered. She told me how her thoughts began subsiding and she had more quiet space between them. She enjoyed the experience and how it centered and grounded her. She saw the benefit in being able to access this piece of mind by tapping into Source or The Tao/Wu Chi before communicating with people.

"To touch the soul of another human being is to walk on holy ground."
—Stephen R. Covey

The Way of Effortless Leadership

Our Third Conversation

We began discussing **Spring – Cultivating Culture.** Natasha said that she had been practicing her meditation twice a day since our last conversation and felt a calmness she had never felt before. She said she realized how much of what had happened in that experience had come out of her own past programming, anxiety, fear, and judgment. She saw how her vibrations had been communicated to her people on a daily basis. She said that if she had maintained the internal stillness from meditation and kept the focus on her own awareness and self-cultivation, she wouldn't have come across as a "bulldozer" and created a culture of "fear and distrust." She realized that she shut down her people's ability to think and communicate clearly by being distrustful, impatient, and restless. If she were to do it again, she would have modelled her newfound inner peace and self-awareness, sowed a culture of trust and confidence, and encouraged other managers to do the same.

Next, we talked about **Summer – Create and Coach.** Natasha saw that once the culture of confidence, trust, and psychological safety was firmly established, she could then nurture it by putting her attention on summer and creating what needed to be done to support the culture. This is the time she would have introduced her new initiatives, like summer hours and more fun activities, as they would have been received as authentic ways to contribute to a more trusting, fun, and adult culture. In this stage, she would coach people by being quiet, enthusiastic, asking them their opinions, and getting them to problem-solve their own issues without providing them with the answers. During this, she would remain aware of her own reactions and behaviour. She would be still, keep the focus on her own self-cultivation, be aware and sensitive to her people's developmental needs, and address issues quickly before they got out of hand. This would have sent a better, warmer, and clearer signal to her people. She would see herself as a coach, a servant leader who was there to facilitate each of her people's growth. She would find out their personal and professional goals and look for ways to provide them with more opportunities to learn and challenge their skills.

Natasha saw that if she had put her focus on her own and other people's development, this would have built a foundation of deep trust and communication, and that in challenging times, she could ask for her people's help in tackling the challenge together in **Late**

Summer – Change. She realized that closing her door to "get work done" was wrong and if she were to do it again, she would spend even more time communicating, allowing her people to share their feelings and ideas and to commiserate and collaborate to tackle the mutual goal. She would have put more focus on maintaining rapport and building the culture of trust, openness, and confidence before trying to implement new initiatives. When change and the hard economic times hit, instead of spending less time, she would have spent more time just being with and coaching her people to ensure their psychological safety, energy, and engagement remained high so they could remain in a productive state of flow.

Lastly, we delved into **Fall – Consolidate Learning**, as the sales results came in, Natasha said she would continuously collect information regarding her own self-cultivation and way of being with her people. She would have a 360 degree evaluation (where her people review her performance) and use the information to see where she was succeeding and where she needed to improve and self-cultivate.

PART FOUR:
FLOW

Chapter 11 – How to Surf Flow – Meditation in Activity

In Taoism, the goal is to get in sync with the flow of the universe.

> *"Be the stream of the universe"* —<u>Tao Te Ching</u> (28), Lao Tzu

Using the "model" of the Way in Chapter 9 will allow you to enter the state of flow more frequently. This section of the book will provide more insight into Taoist concepts to help you create conditions conducive to entering flow.

You, like all leaders, dream of having a fully engaged workforce of people who are performing at the best of their ability. However, many leaders unintentionally act in a way that takes people out of the state of optimal effortless performance frequently called "flow."

> *"Those who flow as life flows know they need no other force."*
> —Lao Tzu

Have you ever been so completely engaged and immersed in an activity or an experience that you lost self-awareness and awareness of surroundings and time, an experience where "you," that is, your ego or judging self disappeared and you became the activity? Maybe it was working on a project, playing a sport or an instrument, or playing with your kids. This state is similar to a spiritual experience that usually correlates with peak performance. Tai chi masters refer to this experience as "flow." Mihaly Csikszentmihalyi's book *Flow: The Psychology of Optimal Experience* defined the experience. Athletes call it being in the "Zone." In my experience, flow is meditation or mindfulness while in activity.

The experience of flow is directly related to self-cultivation because the Taoists believe that all you need to do is get in flow with nature's way. This chapter and the ones that follow will provide you with more areas to cultivate within yourself that will allow you to let go and fall into nature's stream of consciousness, and experience more joy in your life and work.

When I enter a state of flow while performing an activity, I feel relaxed, more aware of everything around me, in control, and use just the right amount of effort (Wu Wei). Afterwards, I feel joyful with a sense that I've grown. I also feel that I went beyond my normal

The Way of Effortless Leadership

experience of life and tapped into something larger. In flow, I'm not aware of myself; I'm just completely into the activity or the person. Life seems beautiful, fluid, and connected. Nothing is forced and everything happens easily.

The flow of life has a natural wave-like cycle. It flows and can't be rushed, altered, or stopped. It's a sea of never-ending ebb and flow of waves. Everything starts in the same source, nothingness/oneness (Wu Chi), is born, differentiates itself, grows, changes (Tai Chi), and eventually returns to source or oneness (Wu Chi). We don't always know when the wave will crash, so we have to be aware, sensitive, and not fight it. It's impossible to make anything last forever; all we can do is get in flow with our experience and use nature's force to take us on our journey.

Think of yourself as a surfer. You need to be relaxed, aware, and attuned to the environment. You must catch the wave of flow. The surfer respects nature's power and seeks to get in flow with the wave for a while. Balancing on the board is incredibly difficult because of the unpredictable changes in the waves. You have to be completely present and sensitive to what's happening. You can do incredible feats with the help of the waves of change, but you're constrained by the timing, power, and direction of the wave. If you go against it, you'll get slammed into the surf.

Stop Trying so Hard; Just Be Present and Do

Paradoxically, the harder you try to hold onto the experience of flow, keep it alive, and control it, the faster it disappears and the less enjoyment you'll have in it. Just as if you grasp fine sand tightly, it will sift through your fingers, but if you cup your hand gently, you can keep it in the palm of your hand. When you get too focused, you lose a broader awareness that's necessary for flow to occur. The more you enjoy the moment, the better you can anticipate, feel, and ride the wave and have a sense of control.

Let Go of Your Ego and Attachment to Results

I learnt this lesson from my dad when I was playing tennis as a teen. I loved the sport and practiced for hours every day. I was so intent on improving and proving my skill but wasn't having the results I wanted in tournaments. One day, my dad said something that didn't seem to make sense at the time:

"You care too much about the results. Focus on enjoying the game."

Being the typical teen, his words of wisdom went in one ear and out the other. A few years later, I looked back, reflected, and realized he was right. He had been speaking about the Buddhist concept of **"Nonattachment"** in different terms. I saw that I had lost the enjoyment of my sport because of my obsessive goal-oriented focus. My attachment was to my ego, looking good, and getting good results. This obsession made my body tense and prevented my body-mind-spirit from working as a relaxed, unified whole. It had narrowed my awareness and took me out of the present moment, which is essential in responding to the ever-changing game. I began experimenting with this "too simple" approach, and my results greatly improved. Best of all, I noticed that I had more fun and regained my love of the game. I ended up teaching tennis in university and became aware that I loved to help people learn. In time, this led me to career and life coaching people, as I wanted to help them self-actualize.

Nature and people resist being controlled. The ego believes, ironically, that it's "not worthy" because it's separate from all else and, therefore, must try to control the situation. You cannot effectively force learning, change, or results. If you try to, you immediately create internal or external stress and resistance. Learning, change, growth, and results are a process that has its own timeline. The best you can do is to create optimal conditions for them to learn and perform. So, you can relax, realize nature's way, and get in flow with it, or you can deny it, use all your might to resist it, and frustrate yourself. The best and most enjoyable way to deal with it is to let go, be aware of the present moment, and use nature's force. This is when you transcend yourself and reconnect with nature.

"Train yourself to let go of everything you fear to lose." —Yoda

Flow is a creative experience that provides a sense of discovery and pushes people to new levels of performance, self-realization, and states of consciousness. It's a joyous feeling where you feel you're giving everything you have to accomplish the task.

Bill Scanlon, professional tennis player who reached a #9 ranking in the world (1970s and 1980s), in his and Dr. Joe Parent's book *Zen Tennis* recounts the experience of being in flow or what they call being in the zone when he became the first man to win a "golden

The Way of Effortless Leadership

set." For those who don't play tennis, it means he didn't lose a single point during the six-game set.

> *While I was in it, I wasn't the least bit self-conscious about being in it. It felt that nothing was blocking my ability to perform at the highest level. The Zone was not some place I had found; it was more like it found me... was relaxed and calm. Everything seemed to flow effortlessly. I was not trying to concentrate, yet I was naturally focused and present. It seemed that I was allowing the shots to happen all by themselves, without any conscious effort on my part (and certainly no thought of mechanics or technique). I was letting it happen, rather than making it happen. Everything seemed very simple, and I had a clarity of purpose without much mental chatter. I saw things very clearly; so much so that it was as if I knew where my opponent was heading and where I would hit it before it happened...In addition to the clarity of vision, there was an extended sense of time. It wasn't exactly like we were moving in slow motion, but there was a feeling that there was no need to rush to get the ball and produce the return I intended...At times, I felt that I was watching myself play from a place outside my own body, like I was watching myself from above and slightly behind. I could see what I was going to do before I did it."*

One can't force flow to happen but you can optimize the possibility of it occurring by creating the necessary climate/culture/conditions. Structured activities like work, sports, games, and learning a musical instrument work well. Create a "game" where your employees can be challenged and have a realistic chance to win.

Flow is about losing your sense of self while being engaged in the activity. **Making someone feel self-conscious, nervous, tense, or anxious at work will backfire and just prevent them from entering this highly productive state.** So, if you want to help your people get into flow:

- Demonstrate you trust them by providing them space, getting out of their way, and intervening less. Don't micromanage.
- Make sure they can realistically complete the task with their level of ability. Provide them with further training if needed.

- Help them set their own realistic goals but don't obsess about them.
- Allow process to take its course and inform and change goals or the path to the goal.
- Smile.
- Show that you don't take yourself so seriously. Use appropriate humour to lighten the mood and create an environment of relaxation.
- Teach your people how to meditate.
- Use Wu Wei and teach your people how to use Wu Wei.
- Allow them to self-manage and control their own work and time.
- Give them a quiet place so they can concentrate on what they're doing.
- Coach them and provide them with immediate feedback.

In the following chapters, you'll learn how to use other principles, ideas, and techniques to have a better chance of entering and staying in flow.

The Way of Effortless Leadership
Chapter 12 – Use Yi, Forceless Intention

In both tai chi and yoga, the use of effortless intention or what the Chinese call "yi" is important in following nature's way. Relaxed intention is the mental state that unites yin and yang and allows creativity and innovation. Using yi gives you the best chance of entering a state of flow. Each life form has instincts and clear desires or intentions but uses the minimal amount of effort, Wu Wei, to get there. Think of a tree root that encounters an immovable boulder; it goes around it. Achieving things in life is almost never a straight line. Life, as do goals, requires awareness, intention, and readjustment.

Before anything comes into existence, first there's an idea. Tell yourself you'd like to touch your nose with your right pinky finger. Do it. You have the thought first and accomplish it without struggle or strain. You've developed a level of mastery with your muscles that a toddler doesn't have. So, using yi in leadership will take time and practice.

In tai chi, you use a clear mental intention while trying to achieve your goal with heightened sensitivity, awareness and the least amount of effort. You must be centered within yourself before using it. People starting tai chi use too much concentration, effort, and muscle and tire themselves out. Their bodies and minds don't work as one integrated whole. Older masters who've been doing tai chi for many years conserve their energy, use it efficiently, and can outlast much younger opponents/partners. This seems counterintuitive in our Protestant work ethic Western culture that pushes people to work harder and longer, not more efficiently.

So, always create a clear and relaxed intention, open your awareness, and become sensitive and responsive to everything around you. Let go; trust your body and mind to achieve the goal. Don't force. Don't over- or under-extend. Forcing and over-extending yourself will take you out of a sense of flow. It takes time and practice to become sensitive to what's the right amount of energy, but use your body and mind as gauges. If you feel tense and mentally or physically exhausted, you're not using yi (intention), you're using force. Note that if you're using too little energy, you're also not using yi. There's a fine balance between using too much and too little energy, and each situation is different.

Coach your people to use yi and have them monitor their own energy expenditure. At an optimal level, you should feel energized, peaceful, blissful, relaxed, and aware, not tired, lethargic, angry, or anxious. Your people's results and performance will improve and so will their individual and collective health. Have coaching conversations and team meetings around this concept.

Set a clear goal in your mind. Maintain good will, loving kindness, and aim to do no harm. Hold the image softly in your mind and then work to find the path of least resistance to achieve it.

The Way of Effortless Leadership
Chapter 13 – Play

"In every real man a child is hidden that wants to play."
—Friedrich Nietzsche

Play is an important part of my philosophy of performance and creativity and has been a big part of my life. My wife Tricia encouraged me to include this chapter in the book.

On our property, I watched young animals in nature. They play to explore the world and to learn about life and relationships. Our dog Mardi has distinctive energy and poses she takes to signal when she wants to play.

In the article "The Key to Happiness: A Taboo for Adults?" in the *Huffington Post*, January 18, 2011, Joe Robinson quoted psychologist and cultural explorer Bradford Keeney: "The whole culture is suffering from over conscious intentionality, over seriousness, overemphasis on productivity and work."

Joe Robinson wrote,

> Contrary to stereotype, engaged play is the gateway not to time-wasting but to times that let you contact deeper realms…Play satisfies core self-determination needs, such as autonomy and competence…when you're stressed, the brain's activated emotional hub, the amygdala, suppresses positive mood, fueling a self-perpetuating cycle of negativity. Play can break you out of that straightjacket. It also cuts through stagnation at the office. Studies show that playfulness can increase performance on the job and stoke creativity by breaking up the mental set that keeps us stuck. It resets the brain… This tonic we write off as trivial is a crucial engine of well-being. In its low-key, humble way, play yanks grownups out of their purposeful sleepwalk to reveal the animating spirit within. You are alive, and play will prove it to you.

Psychiatrist and author Dr. Stuart Brown created the National Institute of Play. It "unlocks the human potential through play in all stages of life using science to discover all that play has to teach us about transforming our world."

Dr. Brown, in his TED Talk, discussed the importance of play, even within inter-species mammals. He shows photos of a twelve-hundred-pound polar bear approaching two leashed huskies with predatory body language, ready to attack and have them for dinner. One of the huskies adopts a play bow stance that all dogs use. This signal changed the bear's mind and intent and the two animals start playing and being affectionate with each other. Brown worked with serial killers and claimed most had been deprived of the opportunity to play as a child. Brown claims the opposite of play isn't work but depression.

Play helps us develop:
- Awareness
- Emotional expression and regulation
- Confidence
- Creativity
- Our problem-solving ability
- Social skills
- Cognitive flexibility
- Creative performance
- Passion
- Perspective. Light-heartedness
- Cooperative spirit that leads to team work

Watch Stuart Brown's video on the importance of play.[14]

An attitude of play and fun are a large part in tai chi chuan push hands. This attitude relaxes the body and makes it more aware, balanced, sensitive, and responsive to change. They adopt the Buddhist "beginner mind." Try cultivating a playful attitude within yourself.

Can you come out and play?

Does the above question make your mind drift back to younger days? Can you see your friend's face? Can you recall a more innocent time of possibility when you were more inquisitive, daring, and excited about the future? Your friend simply wanted your company and to share exploration, experience, and learning.

Can you come out and play?

The Way of Effortless Leadership

Doesn't it feel good to hear that question? Why? Because it:

1. involves and engages the whole you: body, mind, and spirit
2. is often outside in nature and makes you feel alive
3. makes you feel accepted and valued/appreciated for simply being you
4. makes you feel connected
5. sounds fun
6. sounds relaxing
7. conjures up anticipation and excitement of the unknown
8. foreshadows the likelihood of new learning, adventure, and discovery
9. is a sincere invitation, something you can accept or turn down, not like most invitations that have a coercive underbelly (especially at work)
10. doesn't make you feel judged
11. is "play" not "work." We look at the activity with a different lens or expectation.

What distinguishes work from play? Work for you might be play for me. It's how you position the activity and how you approach the activity. Your attitude towards what you're doing.

When you think about the difference between play and work, what comes to mind? Fun vs. boredom, spontaneous vs. structured, relaxation vs. stress, free-flowing vs. goal-oriented, acceptance vs. judgment, learning vs. production, the unknown vs. the known, questioning vs. being certain, participation vs. nonengagement, collaborative vs. competitive? List any other distinctions that come to mind.

Kids who play love it because it's natural, organic, fluid, moving, and healthy. If you listen to kids playing in the park or at recess, what sounds do you hear? You probably hear shrieks of laughter, joy, and the sound of high energy. Now, compare that to an adult conversation or meeting. Notice the difference? Adults are quiet, reserved, careful, fearful, and protective, and their energy displays a lack of passion, expressiveness, engagement, and fun.

"Just play. Have fun. Enjoy the game." —Michael Jordan

I remember creating all sorts of made-up games with friends. We created and changed the games in an organic way. The enjoyment wasn't in the winning of the game but in the process of playing, exploring, learning, and interacting with each other. I was fully relaxed, yet deeply aware and attentive to what we were doing.

Why is this important? We're permitted to be ourselves and create without strict rules. We have the permission to fail. We're all learning about self-mastery. We learn a lot about each other. We know that people are more innovative when they're distracted and at play. I believe that those who play together stay together. There's less fighting. There's a common goal to cocreate the game we're playing. There's lots of brainstorming, and great ideas flow. Humour is present. Relaxation is present. Peacefulness is present. It's a transformational experience in which everyone grows and benefits.

> *"We don't stop playing because we grow old; we grow old because we stop playing"* —George Bernard Shaw

Look at how fast children grow, learn, and create. What do they do differently from adults? They move, they play, they experiment, they have fun, they fail, they learn, they don't give up, and they share. Contrast this to most of our workplaces. Notice the difference. It's known that we innovate during times of rest/distraction/play. Einstein was a huge proponent of imagination and was very playful.

> *"The true sign of intelligence is not knowledge but imagination."*
> —Albert Einstein

Imagination flourishes when you play. A fun, playful, and trusting culture helps organizations attract and retain people. It also makes them more satisfied, creative, and customer service oriented because employees love to be there, and customers feel it. Zappos, Google, Twitter, Edelman, and Facebook all realize the value of play.

> *"You can discover more about a person in an hour of play than in a year of conversation."* —Plato

On a scale of 1 to 10, how would you rate the degree of playfulness in your interactions with staff and in the culture in general? The number 1 is being deadly serious with no play, and 10 is being very playful. What could you implement that would encourage more unstructured play at work?

Chapter 14 – Be "Sung," Mentally and Physically Relaxed

In tai chi chuan, being "sung" or having a calm mind, a relaxed loose body and natural breathing are three essentials to health, performance, self-cultivation, and experiencing flow. Maintaining a healthy perspective, keeping a sense of humour, and not taking yourself seriously helps you to achieve this high performance state.

Many of the tai chi warm-ups and qigong exercises are designed to relax the body, mind, and breath. This isn't comatose relaxation but one that allows you to be fully present and aware without being concerned about an internal ache or worry. Being relaxed allows you to have a coordinated and spontaneous response to any force or change coming your way. Sounds easy, but in this busy world, really letting go of internal tension takes lots of practice and discipline. One cannot do tai chi, any sport, or activity at a high level while holding tension in the body or mind. Why? Your body parts cannot work as a unified whole. When your body is tense, it creates a disturbed mind. Being tense also prevents you from being aware and sensitive to what's coming at you from the outside. A relaxed body creates a calm tranquil mind, and this allows you to be keenly aware, agile, and responsive to new vibrations and changing situations. Being sung allows you to build up and circulate your internal qi for optimal health. The body's natural state is relaxation and vibrant health. When it's tense, it creates energy blockages resulting in stress and disease.

In tai chi push hands, beginners discover just how much tension they're holding. When they finally let go of this tension after months or years, the body works as a finely tuned integrated whole. At this advanced stage, you're not muscling one or two parts; your whole body is perfectly coordinated in executing the motion. Relaxing makes you much more sensitive and alive. You can sense what the opponent will do before they act. This natural state uses much less energy because you're doing the minimum amount of effort to achieve the result. Novices get exhausted quickly because they're activating muscles and tendons that don't need to be used. So, relaxation energizes you, makes your more aware, sensitive, compassionate, and responsive.

Cultivating and achieving a state of sung is important not only for the individual but also for teams and organizations to work as a coordinated whole.

I think back to two bosses who had contrasting vibrations and ways of being. They impacted my engagement, productivity, efficiency, and ability to collaborate and serve completely differently. I'll call one Percy. The other was Richard. Both were senior leaders. I've changed a few details.

Percy had worked his way up from the ground floor into a very senior position and was very good at being bottom line, on task, budget-oriented, and tactical. He took himself very seriously. He had an aggressive, angry, and disturbed energy. I once asked him what his vision was, but he couldn't answer the question. He was the furthest thing from being strategic. People were the last thing on his mind and were treated as resources. He kept losing his human resources people. It was a very competitive environment because people felt scrutinized and judged. Percy had little self-control and was often explosive to the point of frightening. His face was usually red, he was badly out of shape, and he looked uncomfortable when he moved. People were afraid of him. Percy hid inside his office most of the day, and when he did emerge, he would often walk around with a tension that was palpable, often without saying anything. He didn't look healthy. He had created an uncomfortable culture where people dreaded seeing him coming. There was no aliveness in the building; people were discouraged from talking to others in different departments; and people became suspicious, defensive, and protective. His inability to relax and create an environment where others could do the same, put me on edge, made me self-aware and worried, and negatively affected my performance and that of others.

Richard was the opposite of Percy. He was bright and convivial but, most of all, relaxed and playful. It was obvious that he felt at ease with himself and didn't have to prove anything. People loved working for him, including me. He didn't take himself too seriously. He almost always had a smile on his face; he was in excellent shape and moved effortlessly like an athlete. He was relaxed, still, and patient. He had been a soldier when he was younger and had been in battle. Maybe his experience of knowing that life is tenuous made him relax and appreciate people more. His way of being made me feel valued, accepted, and appreciated. He was straightforward, honest, and transparent even in difficult conversations. His sense of

The Way of Effortless Leadership

humour was legendary. I remember him teasing me good-naturedly in my first interview. I wouldn't have normally done it, but I teased him back, and this set the stage for our working relationship. Richard's relaxed demeanour put people at ease. He trusted us. He showed interest in everyone personally and professionally. We were more than mere workers or cogs. I was able to focus on the work at hand. It made me want to work hard to make him look good and succeed. It was the time in my career when I was the most creative and productive. My colleagues felt the same, and we had a real sense of confidence in each other and enjoyed collaborating to reach mutual goals. I would often work overtime because I enjoyed the atmosphere and wanted to make a difference to our services and clients.

Take a moment and think back to your own experiences of working with bosses who were either tense or relaxed.

How did they impact your engagement, performance, commitment, and health?

How relaxed are you with yourself and your people?

Are you able to maintain a healthy perspective?

Can you laugh at yourself, or do you take yourself too seriously?

Chapter 15 – Be King "Kong"

In the previous chapter, we discussed the importance of being "sung," having a relaxed mind and body. By relaxing the body and mind, the Chinese aim to achieve a state of mind called **"Kong."** This is a **relaxed state of mind that's empty, free of rigid beliefs about yourself, others, and the world**. Emptying your mind is important in achieving a state of flow.

Why is this state of "Kong" important in business? Well, think about someone who you've had to work with who was the opposite of "Kong." They were unable to see and accept your ideas or information. Their perception was skewed and they couldn't see reality that didn't fit with how they filtered the world. They were "right" fighters, dualistic in their thinking, black was black and white was white. They had a cluttered mind and had rigid ideas of themselves and you. How would you describe your communication with them? It was probably not a very rewarding and productive experience, was it? Their inability to see and accept new, relevant information made them inflexible, judgmental, positional, and tense, and it wouldn't let them be present with you.

Have you ever been in that state of mind opposite of "Kong?" I have, and I don't like the memories because my listening stopped and I unintentionally shut people down. My rigidity put them in this state where they too became rigid and resistant. Any psychologist will tell you that it's an unhealthy psychological state in which to be and can be contagious. At the extreme, this is the cause of both cold and hot wars in the office. Trust, communication, and collaboration are the first victims, followed by health, productivity, and creativity, and, finally, service and success/profit.

"One who is too insistent on his own views finds few to agree with him." —Lao Tzu

Think about how nice it is to have a conversation with someone who's relaxed and free of rigid beliefs about themselves or you. You don't have your guard up. You can relax and be yourself and feel that the person is open. They're secure within themselves and have nothing to prove; they're just exploring and seeking the truth. Their confidence comes from an internal stillness, openness, and desire to learn. You can be that person.

The Way of Effortless Leadership

Being "Kong" helps you:
1. Be present.
2. Improve your awareness.
3. Be sensitive and pick up subtle cues.
4. Accept yours and others' emotions without getting hooked.
5. Accept new information.
6. Be more flexible.
7. Enter a highly productive state of flow.
8. Build trust.
9. Communicate.
10. Collaborate.
11. Improve your mental and physical health.
12. Improve your decision making.
13. Improve your productivity.
14. Improve your creativity.
15. Provide better service.

Accepting new information is key to our growth and evolution.

How do you achieve a state of "Kong?"

1. Adopt a beginner's mind. Let go of the need to be certain and, instead, become curious.
2. Return to Wu Chi by meditating and tap into emptiness (Source).
3. Focus on your breath and get back into your body and out of your head.
4. Review your self-assessment from Chapter 8, "Your Life Lens."
5. Be mindful of your own beliefs, thoughts, and feelings.
6. Don't take yourself so seriously.
7. Look at the big picture and forget the minutiae.
8. Commit to using Wu Wei, effortless effort, and flow with conversations.

Leaders who have rigid mindsets are particularly harmful to organizations, teams, and people because their way of being creates the culture, acts as a model for others, and trickles down to everyone in the workplace.

In Chapter 8, "Your Life Lens," you began to see where your mindset is rigid. Be mindful of where you tense up.

The good news is that you're open to exploring new ways of being because you're reading this book. By making a commitment to cultivate a more "Kong" state of mind within yourself, you'll be the ripple for others in your organization to do the same.

The Way of Effortless Leadership

Chapter 16 – Be "Tzu Jan," Spontaneous and Natural

In Taoism, "Tzu Jan" means the state people or things will achieve (self-realization) if permitted (not blocked) to be natural and spontaneous, so they can be "Zi Ran" or self-so. This is nature's way. Life is expressive and spontaneous and has a course. If you're not spontaneous and natural, you can't enter flow.

Your aim is to focus on building and maintaining relationships and to be as present, natural, and spontaneous as you can be. It requires a relaxed body; a calm mind; and your willingness to be open, transparent, aware, vulnerable, compassionate, and giving.

Being sensitive and listening to your people, stepping back, and getting out of their way are the best things you can do for your people's health and growth and, in turn, your business. You can either facilitate your people's natural evolution by using Wu Wei (effortless action) to coach them or force, control, or coerce them. The latter might work in the short term but will be disastrous in the medium and long term. By creating a culture where people aren't overtly or covertly penalized but encouraged to be themselves, you'll unleash their natural drive, curiosity, engagement, and creativity.

Take time to really get to know your people as complex human beings. Find out how they think, what's important to them, where they want to go, and how they want to develop. Use your yi mind to create an intention that they'll succeed and gently suggest ideas and provide opportunities for them to get there. This takes talent management to a deeper level of personalized individual evolution. If you focus on creating this environment, your people will naturally want to help you accomplish mutual goals, and for the occasional person who doesn't, you can compassionately help them find a more suitable path.

Organizational culture and structure should be designed to encourage people to be themselves (spontaneous and natural), self-develop, and share information while focusing on mutual goals.

Today, there's a lot written about the characteristics of natural leaders. Denise Deluca, in her October 2011 article, *12 Characteristics of a Natural Leader,* first published on BCI's Blog, said, "A natural leader doesn't necessarily intend to lead; others simply feel naturally compelled to follow. (Or put another way: A natural leader doesn't lead, he or she just is, and others just naturally follow.)"

Nature's way is about ease and letting people and things take their natural course. Again, it's all about using the principle of Wu Wei, effortless effort or forceless action.

Chapter 17 – Zhong Din: Keep Moving Stability

In tai chi, being grounded to the earth is important, but **moving stability, "Zhong Din,"** is more important than holding your position. Self-cultivate and move with whatever force is given you. Healthy qi flow stops when you get positional and it becomes sick qi, like stagnant water. When you're positional, you're rigid, both body and mind. When you're rigid, you stop learning, get stagnant, and are easy to break. As a leader, it's important for you to be clear of your core values but hold them lightly and maintain awareness of when you lose your ability to consider new ideas, get rigid, and become immovable. There are times when you need to stand firm on principle, but most of the time, your ego is the problem. As Bruce Lee famously said, "Be water, my friend."

Have you ever had whiplash, a damaged spine, or back or neck pain from an accident? If so, you'll have first-hand knowledge of the importance of maintaining a flexible spine and how debilitating it is to your health and ability to accomplish things when you lose it. Your inability to move freely also affects your thoughts and emotions. Rigid and immovable things can't flow.

Your spine or, more specifically, your spinal canal is a structure that houses and protects your body's information highway, your spinal cord, while enabling your movement in the outer world. Compressed vertebrae force disks to bulge, and the disks press against the spinal cord, interrupting the flow of nutrients and information. Chiropractors work on aligning the body's structure and some will tell you that if the head is properly aligned, the rest of the structure aligns itself naturally. Proper posture and structure of body alignment allows the muscles to naturally relax, and the conscious relaxation of your muscles allows the body to naturally align and less energy and effort is required and less pain is experienced. You're the head of your organization or department. See the connection to Wu Wei? The more relaxed and internally aligned you are as a leader (head) and the less effort you exert, the more naturally your people will relax, your corporate structure and strategies will align, and the more communication will flow. If you, as head, provide undo force to any area on the organizational spine, it will create a misalignment, which will translate into personal, team, and organizational pain.

In Chinese, Ayurvedic, and even Western medicine, anxiety, tension, and stress create ill health and lack of flexibility. The Eastern body-mind-spirit model of health is essential to following the Way.

> *"Men are born soft and supple;*
> *Dead they are stiff and hard…*
> *Thus whoever is stiff and inflexible is a disciple of death*
> *Whoever is soft and yielding is a disciple of life"* —Tao Te Ching
> (76) Lao Tzu

Healthy living things move, bend, and flow in a relaxed fashion in nature. They don't grow stagnant or break. In tai chi, the body needs to be relaxed and the spine flexible to move with the unexpected. The spine is most powerful when it's straight, but it must be able to move freely to adapt to change and bounce back. The same is true of you and your organization. Don't get too fixated on your ego, position, or ideas.

> **"Relaxation is not as easy as it sounds. It involves physical and mental transformation. Physical rigidity always produces mental rigidity and vice versa. Obsessive patterns of thinking accompany repetitive internal tensions."** —Kenneth S. Cohen *The Way of Qigong*

Being "Sung" (relaxed and tranquil) allows qi energy to flow effortlessly throughout the body's structure. Moving encourages energy flow. Bending, stretching, and twisting free up the spine and lubricate the joints so that the spine can move and flow with unexpected changes.

People will refer to someone as having or not having a "spine" or "backbone," speaking about their strength of character and ability to stand their ground. The same is true of an organization; it needs a backbone, which is composed of its core values and structure, to differentiate it and allow it to survive. However, anything done to the extreme becomes a weakness. If someone's spine becomes so rigid and inflexible that they're not able to move, it becomes calcified. The same happens to someone's character or an organization.

You may have heard the term "the sitting disease" where long periods of inactivity create disease within the body and lessen our ability to be in flow with ourselves. People can contract deep leg thrombosis on long haul airline flights from sitting too long. Simply getting up and walking around prevents this from happening. Teams

The Way of Effortless Leadership

and organizations can similarly become rigid with structure, protocol, rules, and ways of thinking and doing.

Help your people by encouraging physical movement throughout the day. Encouraging movement within the office is easy and inexpensive. Consider implementing walking meetings, stretching, and in-person versus online meetings. To really help people's spines, consider offering group yoga and or tai chi classes during the day. They're wonderful ways for people to be together, to let their energy flow without the stress of the daily tasks.

Staying active, doing some form of daily exercise that moves and bends your spine, and breathing deeply will keep all your bodily fluids and qi flowing for optimal health. Also, when you find your center and balance within your body, you find it in your mind. It will help you and your people to think more clearly.

Yoga, tai chi, qigong, and dancing are particularly good because they include a lot of twists and bends, which keep your spine flexible, allowing the energy to move up through your energy centers, opening vertebrae and nourishing the internal organs.

Similarly, your organizational or team structure/way of operation needs to have some structure and rules but it should be designed to allow people to respond easily and freely, or it will stop the free flow of energy, ideas, and information. Fewer rules are better. Creating structure, policies, and practices that allow people to use their best judgment to adapt to changing circumstances and client needs is essential. When the structure can't move, the organization is living for itself and not its clients or people. It becomes dull, heavy, and uninspired. Creating a structure that's based around what people need to feel empowered works.

Living things have sense organs that allow them to respond to internal and external change. An organization needs to create information feedback loops. People are its sensory organs, and what enables them to feedback information to team members, other departments, and leadership is permission, encouragement, and expectation to do so. **Your organizational culture and structure should be based around trust and communication flow.** Trust allows for relaxation. Relaxation allows for all parts of the organization or team to move freely and in sync. Too much structure, too many policies, and too many rules demonstrate a lack of trust in people's ability to make good judgments, be spontaneous, think for themselves, and do the right thing. A flexible structure allows information to flow and nourish all parts of the organization or team. Build the structure around relaxation, flexibility, sensitivity, responsiveness, improving relationships, communication, sharing of information, learning, and flow of energy. Empower people to make decisions. Give them more authority. Enrich their jobs. Tie these elements into your performance management process and use them as competencies on which people will be evaluated.

The Way of Effortless Leadership
Chapter 18 – Be Aware

In addition to using meditation to enter Wu Chi, it's equally important to use awareness during your everyday interactions with people and tasks. Being mindful is the opposite of having a full mind.

Think about driving. What's most important? Noticing everything around you. Keen awareness allows you to arrive at your destination safely. Distracted driving is the cause of most accidents. Keeping your eyes looking far ahead and using your peripheral vision and other senses allows you to deal effectively with any unforeseen change coming your way. Distracted leading results in unsuccessful change initiatives.

The more mindful you become, the less stress you'll experience because you're in the present, fully aware, and not worrying about the past or future. It's like a vacation from your internal chatter. It's exercise for the mind that flexes and develops your mental capabilities. Mindfulness is getting present and realizing what you're perceiving, thinking, feeling, and doing in the moment, right now! It's also about learning what takes you out of being in the NOW. Observe yourself and notice what triggers your monkey mind. Observe what makes you tense up, angry, freeze, or lose patience, perspective, stillness, Zhong Din (stability), and deep connection to another.

You can use any daily activity as part of your mental training. You can practice being fully aware and present during any activity (i.e., answering emails, working on a presentation, having a conversation, playing an instrument, listening to music, walking, reading, sweeping the floor).

Our thoughts, feelings, images, emotions, and sensations come flying into our awareness without us inviting them. The only way to quiet and sometimes stop your thoughts and emotions are to notice them without judgment. Getting hooked by distractions and thoughts of past or future is natural, but the present moment is what's real. The present is the only place you have any direct control or influence. Being mindful is about noticing what you're experiencing, what triggers you, and watching it change in the moment. The more present you can be in business, the better you'll be and perform. Just a word to the wise, don't focus on being present too hard; it won't work as well, and it will take the fun out of it. Keep a relaxed, soft, sensitive, and open awareness. Create an intention to be present, and gently remind yourself if your attention wanders.

My dad, who was a senior executive, had some wonderful sayings. He said to always be aware of how you hold people in your mind.

> ***"Those you like can do no wrong and those you dislike can do no right."*** —My dad, Kenneth Johnston

The more aware and present you can be with someone without your thoughts, opinions, biases, beliefs, and preconceived notions getting in the way, the:
- Clearer and more accurate your perceptions will be of that person.
- Better you can stay in rapport/relationship with that individual.
- Fairer you'll be with everyone.
- More fluid, spontaneous, and appropriate you'll be in any situation.
- Less effort and force you'll use.
- More you'll experience flow.
- Less stressed and more relaxed and at ease you'll be.

Start your self-cultivation in Fall or Winter. Get intimately aware of your blind spots and what triggers you. Be curious about yourself. See yourself as an experiment or case study. Observe your interactions with people, in addition to doing some internal reflection, to uncover:
- Who, when, and what makes your body stiffen or get tense?
- What makes you freeze and lose a feeling of flow?
- What makes you lose your cool/patience and get angry?
- When and in what situations do you hold your breath?
- What makes you lose perspective, flexibility, and get fixated and rigid in your thinking?
- What things trigger you emotionally?
- What makes you lose caring, compassion, and understanding for someone and lose the rapport/relationship with someone?

Your triggers can come from:
- someone's energy
- a place

The Way of Effortless Leadership

- a thought
- a feeling
- an expression or gesture someone makes
- how close someone stands to you
- the sound and volume of someone's voice
- the colour of a person's hair
- the shape of a face
- the smell of perfume
- someone's style of clothing/dress
- the choice of words someone uses
- almost anything

Get clear on when, what, where, and who really triggers you. Write down everything you discover. This is the first part of your self-cultivation and self-awareness. You can't change what you're unaware of. Simply reconnecting to your breath when you notice you're triggered, fixated, or rigid will bring perspective and soften you.

Before starting a conversation:
- Does the person look like someone who hurt or upset you in the past?
- Be conscious of your history with this person.
- What preexisting climate are you bringing to the conversation?
- Be mindful of your history with this person and your thoughts, feelings, opinions, beliefs, and biases about them.
- Be aware of your body and notice if there's any tension.
- Are you fixated on having to make a point or sell some idea?
- How would you characterize your present energy spirit/vibrations?
- Ask yourself if you really want to bring these vibrations to the conversation. If not, can you change them? If you can't, consider having the conversation later.

During a conversation:
- Stay aware of your breath and how your body is feeling. When do you hold your breath and where and when do you tense up in your body? When you feel muscle or mental tension, be quiet, watch your breathing, and sink

it to your lower dan tien (two inches below your navel). This will dissipate stress and tension and kick in your relaxation response.
- Be still.
- Be present.
- Be patient.
- Be interested and give your full attention.
- Be compassionate.
- Expand your awareness of subtleties.
- Ask questions to learn the other person's perspective/worldview. Find out why it's important to them. Really get inside it and forget about your own.
- Listen to understand someone fully, not to find ammunition to prove your point.
- Observe their voice, expressions, and body language.
- If you don't understand something, paraphrase and ask for clarification.
- Observe when your thoughts, feelings, opinions, beliefs, fears, and obsessions take over. When you notice them, acknowledge them inside and then be quiet and return to listening and being present.
- If someone is highly emotional, allow them to have their experience. Maintain a neutral energy, interest, and awareness. Stay or stick with them; don't provide them with any of your own force to use against you. Realize it's about them, not you. Detach from your emotions and reactions, and observe. Don't argue, justify, return the anger, run, etc. Just stay still, observe, keep a neutral face, and let the other person become exhausted. Don't provide fuel for the fire; they'll burn themselves out. This is conversational tai chi push hands. You'll learn more about this in the next chapter.

The last point above is something I discovered by accident. I worked for one executive director who was known to be explosive with everyone under him. I had not personally encountered his temper until one day when he stepped into my office (didn't shut the door, so everyone heard) and just exploded because I had brought up a concern about an issue that I felt would negatively impact our client service. I was so taken aback by the fury and loss of control, that I just stayed silent and watched as his energy dissipated over twenty minutes. I tried to explain, but it was futile. Eventually, he just stormed out. Two day later, he knocked on my door and asked if he

The Way of Effortless Leadership

could talk to me in private. We went into an adjacent office and he apologized and asked if I could forgive him. I said, "Sure; everyone has bad days," and we shook hands. I don't hold grudges. In the coming weeks, I heard him go off on other people. Not too long after, a representative from the board of directors came in and fired him. He wasn't self-aware, aware of his energy on others, and wasn't using Wu Wei.

"To the mind that is still, the whole universe surrenders." —Lao Tzu

Chapter 19 – Use Push Hands Principles to Flow with Change and Conflict

In everyday conflict, people confuse the other person's BEING with the idea or position that person is taking. It becomes a battle of egos, will, strength/force, and dominance or submission. It's like two different universes meeting. People usually square off against each other. They force their points, ideas, and positions on the other. It could be likened to two arrows pointing at each other, blocking or resisting each other's self-expression, or one capitulates, gives up, and retreats. There's tension, lack of understanding, often aggression, and bad feelings afterwards.

One can use the basic principles of tai chi push hands in dealing with and transforming force and conflict in interpersonal relationships. In tai chi chuan push hands, instability, overextending, grasping, rigidity, tension, and inability to feel or be sensitive leads to your defeat because the opponent can use your momentum and stiffness against you. The idea is to meet aggression with softness or empty space. Being relaxed, soft, and sensitive allows you to feel and move your "opponent" with subtlety. The idea is to not give the opponent anything they can use against you and to allow them to provide the energy or force that you'll use. See the End Notes section to see videos of Tai Chi Chuan Push Hands and Forms.[15]

Push hands is the step between doing the slow-moving form and actual martial applications in tai chi chuan.

Practicing push hands teaches us over time how to transcend ego, force, and dominance because trying to use these will work against you when you're giving your opponent energy and momentum that they can use against you. At a high level, there are no prescribed motions, and everything is permitted and spontaneous. It's a playful exercise to allow one to test their mastery of the tai chi principles, and it requires partners. One can't reach this state of mastery by oneself. It's sensitivity training. It's a fun and energetic exercise where two partners/opponents (slowly at first) provide force to the opponent. Using your yi mind, relaxing, and staying grounded (rooted) are essential. One gets to test his or her ability to stay grounded, centered, and neutralize the force without blocking or running, using tai chi principles. Then the "adversary" returns the favour and pushes into the other, giving him the same opportunity.

The Way of Effortless Leadership

Every move has its yin and yang elements and when one pushes, they're yang and when they receive, they're yin. There's no way to learn true martial tai chi without having multiple partners who provide one with a safe way to explore their ability to keep their Zhong Din (dynamic stability) and use Wu Wei (effortless effort).

In mental push hands, you'll use the same goals of **remaining grounded and maintaining dynamic stability.** You'll use the principles of **"nonresistance," "awareness," "sticking," "following," "listening strength or Tin Jin," "sensitivity," "redirecting,"** and **"playing"** skills to feel and understand someone's force/position/ideas to get inside their universe, understand their intention, and allow them to feel yours.

Remember, soft overcomes hard. The idea of play is important to this exercise. It allows both people to enjoy the process of learning without the negative aspects of hyper competition (ego-inflation, domination, aggression, etc.). Both people win because they have a safe place to play, explore, and experiment without negative emotions or tension. You'll see their force as a gift that enables you to develop deeper self-awareness, understanding, cultivation, and skill. You'll join with them in the direction of their force without resistance. You won't pull; you'll just let them push and turn you slightly, as you relax and let them exhaust their pushes.

You and your partner will be starting in neutral "Wu Chi" positions (neither has committed any force or position). You will stay in Wu Chi (no action) and allow your partner to start the conversation and be yang. You will be "soft" or yin, and receive and "listen" to what they have to say or give. When you've understood and felt it, you'll switch to yang and push back with sensitivity, making sure you don't over-extend yourself or push too much. Then, you'll let them come back as you feel out their position. Staying aware, fluid, flexible, and responsive is important. This tai chi play goes on until the end of the conversation and then you aim to return to neutral (Wu Chi) to complete it.

Seeing force and conflict as opportunities for testing your ability to remain stable, calm, centered, rooted, flow with change, and use Wu Wei (effortless effort) will transform the way you view people, conflict, and external change. See your "opponent" as your partner in mutual learning, growth, and transformation.

Breathing naturally is extremely important and **allows your qi to flow.** If you find yourself holding your breath, just observe it, let it go, and **sink it below your navel.**

1. Check your mental and emotional state before engaging someone in conversation, especially when there could be a potential for conflict. Be aware and disengage from any strong emotions or dogmatic views.
2. Notice any rigid positions you hold. Let go mentally of your position.
3. If time permits, close the door, meditate, and tap into Wu Chi.
4. Smile internally at your whole body and, in your mind's eye, smile at the individual with whom you're about to have the conversation.
5. Keep your spine straight, crown pulled up and chin slightly tucked to align your structure and allow your qi to flow. This is called **"Din-Jin" or "erect head, empty neck."** It's essential in keeping the body's equilibrium and is strong, balanced body language.
6. Try not to engage unless you're centered, stable, and can see the valuable BEING behind the worker. Bring caring and compassion to the encounter.
7. Intend to learn more about yourself and the other from this encounter and wish the same for you "opponent" so that you can have a mutually satisfying resolution to the problem, conflict, or issue.
8. Stay relaxed, aware at all times, and use mental intention, not force.
9. Approach your partner as a play partner with whom you'll want to continue playing with after this conflict has been solved. Separate the person from the position. Protect the relationship.
10. Mentally thank them for the force they're bringing. Couple with their force and join them in mutual exploration, learning, and mastery.
11. Protect your partner's well-being at all times. If they get injured you don't have anyone with whom to practice or play.
12. Let them start. Be yin (soft) at first. Accept the other's force or energy by **"listening"** and **"sticking"** to it, following it, sitting back, and taking it in.

The Way of Effortless Leadership

13. Join with their force, taking them in the direction they're going, neutralizing or using **"lu,"** redirecting only when it gets into your center and is about to off-balance you.
14. Once you've fully received what they're giving you, come forth slowly, maintaining your softness and sensitivity with yours to give them a chance to feel and understand it.
15. Don't overextend or retreat; stay centered and slowly test their position with sensitivity with your push or point(s).
16. Maintain a positive spirit throughout. If you get hooked on your position or are trying to force it, your opponent will off-balance you in the direction you're leaning.
17. If you injure someone accidently, apologize immediately.
18. Enjoy the back and forth (yin and yang) movement. Stay present.
19. End with a smile and an internal thank you.
20. Take time afterwards to evaluate what you learnt about the other person and their position. What are your common interests? If the issue wasn't resolved, what was left undone? Resolve to find a way that both of you secure a win.

Below, in an excerpt from an article in *Kung Fu Magazine*, Jonathon Miller, CEO of America Online, discusses the deep insights he's gained from practicing Chen style tai chi (Taiji) and how the principles have helped him as a business leader. Miller gives an example:

> *One should be prepared to move when ready and able. In business, it is most important to see the situation at hand and move as the situation requires. You have to fit yourself to the situation. From my understanding, I believe that is a Taiji approach, as opposed to saying that the (business) problem must be solved my way without looking at the situation for what it really is at that moment in time.*

Conflict Resolution Push Hands

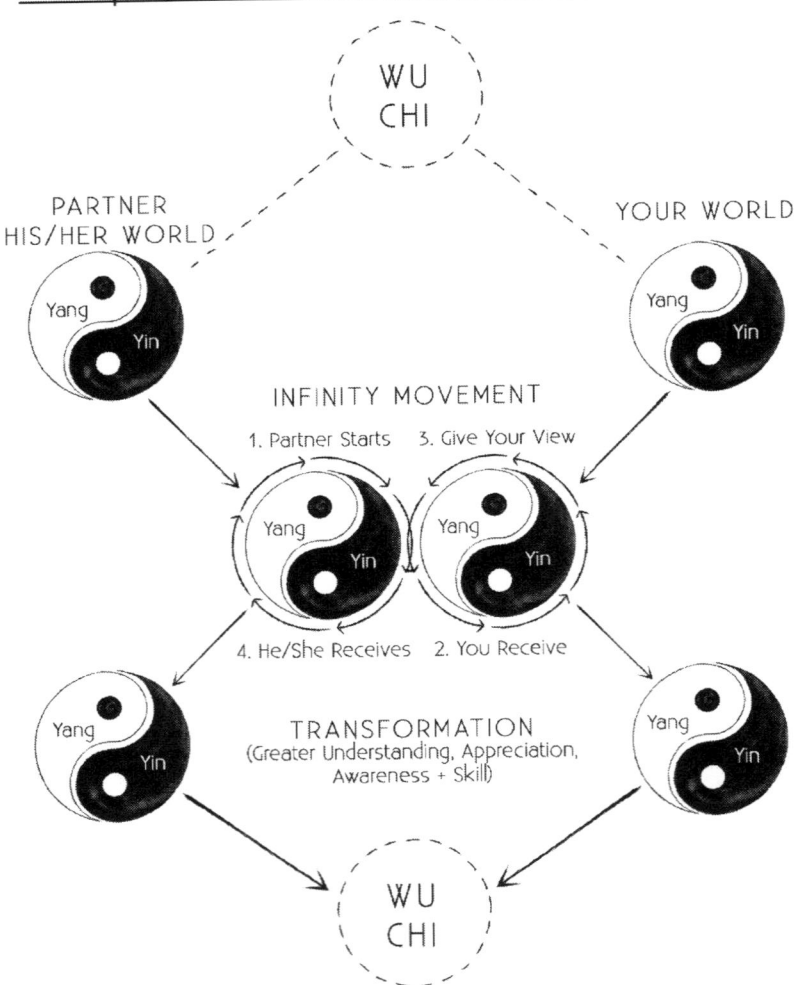

WU CHI

PARTNER HIS/HER WORLD

YOUR WORLD

Yang / Yin

INFINITY MOVEMENT

1. Partner Starts
3. Give Your View
4. He/She Receives
2. You Receive

TRANSFORMATION
(Greater Understanding, Appreciation, Awareness + Skill)

WU CHI

The Way of Effortless Leadership
Chapter 20 – Work with Paradox

Taoism, tai chi, yoga, quantum mechanics, string theory, and nature are all paradoxical, mystical, and counterintuitive but, at the same time, practical. They're paradoxical because you can't force flow; you must let go and allow it to enter you, so you can be carried away by it.

> *"All streams flow to the sea because it is lower than they are. Humility gives it its power. If you want to govern the people, you must place yourself below them. If you want to lead the people, you must learn how to follow them."* —Lao Tzu, Tao Te Ching

Our overattachment or identification with our ego, ideas, people. and things is the problem. We see ourselves as separate. Everything is black or white in our thinking. But, this isn't the way in nature. Yin always has some yang in it and yang always some yin. Front and back are just two sides or perspectives to the same reality. Reality isn't rigid and positional; it's flowing, relational, and playful.

In quantum mechanics, an electron/photon (light) is both a wave and a particle at the same time. Life, at the deepest level, operates naturally as waves, but when someone observes it, it shows up as particles or matter. Our attention or consciousness changes its state and how it appears. Just as with awareness, intention and expectation you bring to a project or a conversation will change how it shows up to you.

String theory and quantum mechanics believe that it's highly probable that multiverses exist and that our existence is like a hologram, in which we're like avatars and get to try out different actions and have different results simultaneously.

Taoism shows us that many paradoxical lessons from nature exist that we would be wise to heed. The five that I think are the most relevant are: 1) be soft to be strong, 2) yield to hold steady, 3) lead from behind, 4) go slow to go fast, and 5) let go to gain control.

1) Be Soft to Be Strong

Being soft and caring with your people will make you seem strong in their eyes.

"Water is fluid, soft and yielding. But water will wear away rock, which is rigid and cannot yield. As a rule, whatever is fluid, soft and yielding will overcome whatever is rigid and hard. This is another paradox: what is soft is strong." —Lao Tzu

2) Yield to Hold a Steady Position

Letting go of the need to be right, listening, and being flexible to the winds of change is a sign that you're flowing with nature's course, and this will allow you to be healthy, survive, and thrive.

"A tree that is unbending is easily broken." —Lao Tzu

3) Lead from Behind

Leading people can be challenging because people don't want to be managed or controlled. That's their human nature. Deep humility is an important quality to cultivate within you. Prideful self-promotion and credit taking makes people resist and not want to give their best because they feel used and disrespected. The only way to bring out a person's natural drive, creativity, and desire to perform is to step back, put them ahead, see them as fully capable, trust them, give them space, and let them step forward and surprise you.

The two following chapters from the *Tao Te Ching* speak to how to lead by following and using humility, paradox, and Wu Wei (effortless action):

> 17
> **"The highest rulers, people do not know they have them**
> The next level, people love them and praise them
> The next level, people fear them
> The next level, people despise them
> If the rulers' trust is insufficient
> Have no trust in them
> Proceeding calmly, valuing their words
> Task accomplished, matter settled
> The people all say, "We did it naturally"

> 66
> "Rivers and oceans can be the kings of a hundred valleys
> Because of their goodness in staying low
> So they can be the kings of a hundred valleys
> Thus if sages wish to be over people

The Way of Effortless Leadership

They must speak humbly to them
If they wish to be in front of people
They must place themselves behind them
Thus the sages are positioned above
But the people do not feel burdened
They are positioned in front
But the people do not feel harmed
Thus the world is glad to push them forward without resentment
Because they do not contend
So the world cannot contend with them"

4) Go Slow to Go Fast

In tai chi, one trains slowly at first to go fast later. Even my tennis coach Dennis Van Der Meer, who trained me to teach tennis, had us play as slowly as possible as a training exercise. He made the point that if we could stroke the ball slowly, that we had positioned ourselves appropriately, and were ready and not rushing. Taking it slowly allows one to be aware and to be able to sense subtleties and ingrain learning at a deeper level. It flies in the face of the current belief that speed allows one to gain the upper hand in this era, but there are so many examples of leaders introducing too many strategies, initiatives, changes, and technologies too quickly and failing miserably. Going slowly at the beginning allows people to work out bugs, relax, build confidence, and go faster in the medium and long term.

5) Let Go to Gain Control

People don't like to be forced to do something against their nature. More trust and less interference allow people's drive and energy to emerge naturally. The concept of Wu Wei, effortless effort, means that one stays consciously engaged, lets go, and becomes one with nature's flow and helps others realize their own nature (Zi Ran). By doing so, one succeeds without trying hard.

Let go. Aim to be more aware and do less. Be still, humble, patient, less impressive, and work quietly in the background to cultivate trust.

These paradoxes are the antithesis of our Western value system of having to be brash, ego/power-focused, and neurotically industrious. So, be patient with yourself and realize it will take self-awareness and practice to understand and use this treasure. Let go and allow nature's flow to enter you.

The Way of Effortless Leadership

Chapter 21 – Use the Science of Compassion

"When a man moves away from nature his heart becomes hard."
—Lakota Proverb

The three gifts of wisdom Lao Tzu offers us are compassion, simplicity, and patience. This chapter speaks to the first and the following chapters to the last two.

My years as a consultant have taught me that this is THE one area where many leaders have the most improvement to make. Many leaders still believe that being tough-minded and "objective" is the mark of a good leader and that "soft" and "fuzzy" feelings have no place in business and should be reserved for one's personal life. Many still feel that showing care and compassion shows weakness. They tend to treat people as things or resources necessary to complete tasks and goals. They believe that the best way to motivate their people is to create a high-pressured competitive environment and test them in a baptism of fire. The focus on task accomplishment and the ability to make "cool," "objective" decisions are often the only considerations and seen as the mark of a good leader.

However, research now shows that compassion, caring, and kindness improves a multitude of business markers and goals. Harsh, noncompassionate leaders trigger the fight, flight, or freeze response in people, making them self-conscious, taking them out of flow. A warm, caring, compassionate leader greatly reduces the fear in the culture, lets people relax, be less self-concerned, and enter a state of flow.

> **"And the men who hold high places**
> **Must be the ones to start**
> **To mold a new reality**
> **Closer to the heart"**
> —Rush, "Closer to the Heart"

Look back at "Your Life Lens" self-assessment exercises from Chapter 8. I'll bet that most of you described your best bosses as compassionate, kind, or caring. In fact, empathy and compassion are necessary for good mental health.

Our own mistaken belief that we're separate from each other, animals, and nature and can't make a difference works against us cultivating our natural compassion. We try to feel better about ourselves by differentiating ourselves and feeling superior. Psychologists know that narcissism has been steadily increasing. To turn the tide, we need to begin by ceasing our harsh criticism. Criticism demotivates us because it triggers the fight, flight, or freeze response.

Jon Ronson, British journalist, who wrote the book *The Psychopath Test: The Journey Through the Madness Industry* was interviewed by Jeff Bercovici of *Forbes Business* in an article "Why (Some) Psychopaths Make Great CEOs." His research shows that psychopathy is four times greater in CEOs than in society at large. Ronson said:

> I think my book offers really good evidence that the way that capitalism is structured really is a physical manifestation of the brain anomaly known as psychopathy.
>
> A really interesting question is whether psychopathy can be a positive thing. Some psychologists would say yes, that there are certain attributes like coolness under pressure, which is sort of a fundamental positive. But Robert Hare would always say no, that in the absence of empathy, which is the definition in psychology of a psychopath, you will always get malevolence.
>
> Basically, high-scoring psychopaths can be brilliant bosses but only ever for short term. Just like Al Dunlap [one of *Time Magazine*'s Top 10 Worst Bosses], they always want to make a killing and move on.
>
> And then you've got this question of what came first? Is society getting more and more psychopathic in its kind of desire for short-term killings? Is that because we kind of admire psychopaths in all their glib, superficial charm and ruthlessness?

Looking at the extreme end of the spectrum, what is one of the first warning signs that a child may become a serial killer? They torture animals. They completely lack empathy and compassion for other beings and treat them as things or toys for their perverted amusement. To use the Way and unify with nature, it's important to feel the suffering of animals and humans.

The Way of Effortless Leadership

Buddhists have long practiced compassion as contemplative neuroscience to self-cultivate, reduce suffering, and improve happiness and health. They do a meditation based on compassion.

> *"Basic human nature is gentleness. We are equipped with the seed of compassion"* – the Dalai Lama

Let me share a personal story that highlights this fact. Many years ago, my girlfriend at the time, her young children, and I were out walking in downtown Toronto. We had given the kids some money to spend on themselves. We passed a homeless man. The children stopped walking and asked us if they could give their money to the man. We told them, "If you do, you won't have any for yourselves." They both chose to give the man their money. They beamed with delight the whole day.

In Adrian F. Ward's article in *Scientific American* on November 20, 2012, "Scientists Probe Human Nature – and Discover We Are Good, After All," he points to seven experiments using 2,068 participants and says, "Recent studies find our first impulses are selfless."

Businesses are just waking up to the benefits of developing compassionate leadership and cultures as the costs of stress (heart disease, anxiety, depression, turnover, lack of engagement, and low productivity) are skyrocketing. Businesses that put a focus on creating a compassionate culture enjoy better customer service; increased productivity, loyalty, retention, and employee satisfaction; and improved collaboration and creativity.

Compassion, caring, and kindness are essential to the Way. Compassion is the sun that warms the earth and is necessary for growth. If you cultivate it within yourself and your leadership team, it will uplift everyone's spirits and spread like wildfire throughout the culture.

In addition to reducing financial costs, compassion:

- Makes us happy
- Allows us and others to enter an optimal state of flow
- Creates greater motivation

- Improves performance by reducing stress
- Positively affects the brain's development
- Improves everyone's health, well-being, and lifespan
- Reduces damaging inflammation that leads to a multitude of illnesses
- Counteracts depression
- Improves relationships and sets the ground for collaboration
- Makes us more attractive

Cultivating compassion within yourself and your organization is a very inexpensive way to positively impact your company's bottom line.

Most of all, being more compassionate will transform your own experience of work. You'll look forward to coming to work and being around happy people who are deeply grateful and loyal.

Start with yourself. Begin by forgiving yourself and appreciating yourself and then throw a wide net of compassion over all those that you touch. Buddhists train in broadening their compassion for all sentient beings, including animals on our planet. If you're interested in broadening your compassion, visit your local Buddhist centre, or type into YouTube search: Guided Compassion Meditation.

"There is a battle of two wolves inside us all.
One is evil. It is anger, jealousy, greed, resentment, lies, inferiority, and ego.
The other is good. It is joy, peace, love, hope, humility, kindness, empathy, and truth.
The wolf that wins? The one you feed." – Cherokee Proverb

The Way of Effortless Leadership
Chapter 22 – Use Simplicity and Clarity

"Simplicity is the ultimate sophistication."
—Leonardo Da Vinci

Complexity creates confusion for people and overwhelms them.

Nature grows from simple.

My father was a senior executive with a large insurance company before he retired. He always said that great design is simple. Good communication is clear.

Less is more.

Decide what your core message is and then put it through a filter of simplicity. Remove all excess.

Take time up front to think about what initiatives will create the greatest leverage to achieve your goals. If possible, keep them to one or two.

Use common everyday language.

Eliminate bureaucracy.

When people see a worthy goal clearly and know it's attainable, it motivates them.

"Any intelligent fool can make things bigger and more complex; it takes a touch of genius and a lot of courage to move in the opposite direction." —Albert Einstein

Chapter 23 – Use Patience

Nature is patient. You can't rush it, yet it always produces incredible growth. This year, in British Columbia, spring came two months late, but it came.

Leaders always seem to think that growth can be continuous. This is unnatural. If you try to push your people to achieve unnatural growth goals, you stress them out and achieve the exact opposite. There are always periods of dormancy in a growth cycle, but after the fall and winter, nature goes wild!

Your people are part of nature. Give them the space and time to grow and produce. They'll feel your patience and will interpret it as trust. Impatient leaders demonstrate they don't trust their people and the process, and this negatively impacts their people's level of engagement.

Notice when you get impatient and ask yourself:

- What triggers it?
- How does your body language change?
- How does your breathing change?
- How do your thoughts change?
- How do your emotions change?
- When you do notice it inside you, just watch it; don't act on it. Let it be, and it will subside.

As you become more patient with yourself and others, observe how their reactions to you change. Notice how their energy and performance changes.

The Way of Effortless Leadership
Chapter 24 – Practice Self-Cultivation Mind-Body Exercises

This isn't a book on yoga, tai chi, or qigong, but practicing these energy arts will reconnect you with nature's way. They'll ground you; give you the experience of flow; make you relaxed and flexible; improve your health, energy, and wellbeing; and transform your level of awareness/consciousness and the "vibes." In turn, your new vibes will be noticed and mirrored by your people and will shift your entire culture.

Yoga, like tai chi and qigong is experiential. You use your mind to get back into your body to allow it to return to its natural state to self-actualize. These arts are designed to remove the tension from your body and invoke the relaxation response.

> *"The relaxation response is a physical state of deep rest that changes the physical and emotional responses to stress...and the opposite of the fight or flight response."* —Harvard Professor of medicine Herbert Benson, *The Relaxation Response*

You'd be surprised by how much tension you hold in your body without being aware of it. You can't fully understand these arts by reading and evaluating them intellectually. You don't need to believe in yoga, tai chi, or qigong; their benefits are testable. I would encourage you to commit to one of these arts for a minimum of one year and practice daily when possible. These mind-body practices will have healing and transformational effects on your body, mind, and spirit. If you're interested in tai chi, consider Wu style, Chen style, Yang style or Sun style. I would recommend that you stay away from any style that's new age.

Tai chi, qigong, and yoga see your body like a tree with roots, like the tree in the movie *Avatar* that shares energy with everything around it. There's a toroidal (donut-shaped) energy field around your body that exchanges energy with your environment that meets at your heart. Your body collects qi or prana energy from the ground to root you and cosmic energy from above to inspire your growth. To grow and flourish, your roots must be strong. These arts see the body and environment interacting as holistic self-regulating energy ecosystems. If you correct the body's energy, nature will take over and create optimal health and wellbeing. Your breath is particularly important in regulating your qi or prana, and yoga, tai chi, and qigong have multiple breathing exercises to help you accomplish this goal.

The Chinese refer to three energy centres or dan tiens: the brain, the heart, and the gut. Back in Chapter 7, The REAL Real World, I mentioned that Taoists who practice qigong and tai chi do inner alchemy or Neidan. It's a process of collecting, circulating, refining, and balancing jing (original reproductive energy that we're born with), qi (life energy), and shen (spiritual energy). If you're interested in learning a simple way to begin inner alchemy, go to ThoughtCo.com and view a March 31st, 2016 article by Elizabeth Reninger titled "Practice the 'Inner Smile.'"

Yoga, tai chi, and qigong teach you how to collect energy from the earth and intentionally move it up through the feet, legs, and spine through energy centers (dan tiens or chakras). They teach you to direct and sink the breath to the lower dan tien, or chakras, to center and ground you. *Chakra* in Sanskrit means 'wheel.' Intention and breath are used to circulate qi throughout the body through meridians or nadis. The Sanskrit root of *nadi* is *nad* and means 'movement.' Each chakra has its own associated gland or organ; colour; sound; psychological, emotional, and spiritual purpose; and vibrational and musical note. All chakras collect and emit energy. Meditation, sound, and music, in addition to the physical postures and movements of tai chi and yoga, work wonders to clean and balance your energy. Tibetan singing bowls work, in the same way, through vibrations that attune or entrain your chakras.

In yoga and tai chi, there are energy pathways, nadis, or meridians in the body. Yoga has seven main chakras or energy vortexes and the power is stored in your sacral chakra. These vortexes are gates that allow cosmic energy/consciousness from the universe to flow down through your crown chakra, and earth activating energy to flow up through the root chakra. The energies from above and below weave along the spine in different directions and unite in the centre at the heart chakra. The heart chakra is about love, compassion, balance, and acceptance, and it plays a central part in all Eastern systems. White light seen through a prism has all the colours and vibrations that correlate to the various chakras.

Yoga and tai chi see physical, intellectual, and spiritual realization or cultivation as one interrelated process. It's your energy ecosystem. To achieve higher states, you must still the mind, control your breath,

The Way of Effortless Leadership

and balance yin and yang and the five elements. These five elements in both yoga and Taoism (tai chi) correspond to various organs and chakras in your body. You can do too much or too little physical or mental work. You can have too much or too little energy in a chakra or an organ and this imbalance can create mental, emotional, or physical ill health. Think of it as similar to Maslow's hierarchy of needs. Maslow believed that someone could only become self-realized when he or she had lower-level needs met. Chakras in the body relate well to Maslow's hierarchy. In yoga, as we learn to raise our energy vibration up our spine, we reach higher levels of ability, self-realization, and consciousness.

A healthy mind, body, and spirit are all essential for self-realization; one affects the others holistically. I encourage you to begin your own yoga or tai chi practice as part of your self-cultivation and provide opportunities for your people to practice it as well. If yoga classes at work aren't possible, you can teach your people simple meditation and pranayama (breathing exercises) they can do on their breaks. A simple and very effective way to clean and balance the energy in the body is alternative nostril breathing or "nadi suddhi" (it only takes four or five minutes). Go to YouTube and type in "nadi suddhi" to find several videos on how to perform this simple calming breathing exercise.

Your people can feel the energy that's emitted from your energy centers. Having your employees practice meditation and do yoga will not only help everyone become the best they can be (Zi Ran) but will also create the evolution of the organization.

Chapter 25 – Mastery

George Leonard's book *Mastery* changed my view on happiness, skill, and performance. This chapter is a very short summary of his work and how to use it to flow with the Way. He believes that modern society works against mastery by its promises of instant gratification.

I left this topic till the end because it's so critical to be able to use the Way of Effortless Leadership successfully.

The Way of Effortless Leadership is simple, but its beauty lies in your ability to become more aware, mindful, and conscious, and it will allow you to grasp deep wisdom and subtleties that most leaders will never enjoy. Adopting a mastery mindset is critical for you to use and gain the benefits of the Way. When you stumble and falter, you'll be able to quickly notice it and self-correct. Mastery is simple and joyful but not always easy, and here's why.

Mastery isn't perfection, a destination, or reserved for only the especially gifted. It is available to everyone and is an ongoing process.

"At the heart of it, mastery is practice. Mastery is staying on the path."
—George Leonard from *The Life We are Given: A Long-term Program for Realizing the Potential of Body, Mind, Heart, and Soul*

Railing against the frustration and boredom of the learning dip or plateau (no observable progress) is the main reason people fail to master anything. When this happens, most give up, let their monkey mind distract them, and move on to something else. They don't realize that after every learning dip or plateau, they'll jump to a higher skill level and that this process continues indefinitely. In the last few years, I took up the guitar, something I'd fantasized about learning since I was 14. I spent hours each week trying to get my fingers to move where my brain was telling them to go. In the first year and a half, I still couldn't move from chord to chord quickly or strum. I would ask my wife if she could tell what song I was playing. She always furrowed her brow, made a half smile, and said no. Then, one day, seemingly out of the blue, everything started to work together. I relaxed, and the quick changes and the strumming just worked. If I had given up the day before, I would have lost out on the

The Way of Effortless Leadership

joy of playing. The brain and body need time to assimilate information, and that's what happens on the plateau. Looking foolish and getting worse temporarily is necessary to progress.

So, to master anything, you need to:
- Cultivate patience within yourself.
- Let go of perfectionism and the drive to control.
- Play and have fun.
- Use your yi mind to set an intention.
- Relax, learn to love the plateau, go with the flow, and enjoy the journey.
- Practice for the joy of the experience and not for reaching your goal. Paradoxically, the more you can let go of goal fixation, the more you'll relax, use Wu Wei, and the better you'll perform and the sooner you'll reach your goal.
- Mr. Leonard encourages us to realize that resistance to change is normal. All bodies and ecosystems operate on homeostasis to stay healthy. Think of blood pressure, resting heart rate, blood sugar, weight, etc. If one goes above or below specific ranges, ill health or death occurs. Yet, there's room to move within the range. Flow and manage change in a similar fashion. Every system, including us humans, balances the desire to change with the resistance to change. Too much change too fast creates resistance and health problems.
- Don't expect continuous upward progress or growth. Think of making three steps forward, one or two back.

By not expecting perfection and continuous improvement from yourself, you'll naturally relax, and this relaxation will change your energy or vibrations that you give off to your people. Consider providing your people with George Leonard's book *Mastery* and have conversations around this concept, encouraging them to use it.

PART FIVE:
THE WAY IN BUSINESS TODAY

Chapter 26 – Companies That Are Investing in Mind-Body-Spirit Practices

The Way has provided you with both scientific and mystical explanations of why meditation, mindfulness, and energy arts such as tai chi, yoga, and qigong are beneficial for health, growth, realization, and performance.

In David Gelles's book *Mindful Work*, the *New York Times* reporter shares how and why 25% of major U.S. corporations have started to embrace these mind-body-spirit stress reduction practices. In a March 25, 2015 article in *The Atlantic*, Joe Pinkster interviews Gelles. When asked why he thinks mindfulness is taking root in organizations at this time in history, Gelles replies that there are three reasons.

1. Over the last 30 years, there's been this tremendous volume of research. Academic research, scientific research that's really been quantifying the effects of mindfulness. And we can now see it actually changes the structures of our brain in ways that we think are largely positive. It actually improves our immune system in ways that we can verifiably measure. It actually seems to reduce the stress we experience and the stress that our bodies seem to be reporting, through measures like heart-rate variability and cortisol levels. So, the data is there…

2. The second thing I think that has helped is that over the last 30 years, mindfulness has become truly a secular pursuit…

3. The third is, I think mindfulness is being accepted in the workplace today because we need it more than ever, it seems. We're so stressed. We're so bombarded with constant information overload.

The following companies have discovered mind-body-spirit practices:

1. General Mills:
   - Mindful leadership program that uses a combination of Buddhist sitting meditation, gentle yoga, and dialogue to settle the mind. It's

- designed to improve employee focus, clarity, and creativity
- Meditation room in every building
- 89% of executives reported having better listening skills
- 80% of executives reported making better decisions

2. Mckinsey & Company:
   - Embracing meditation as new HR strategy
   - Meditation
   - Self-analysis programs

3. Google:
   - "Search Inside Yourself," a program that teaches employees how to listen to colleagues, breathe mindfully, and improve their emotional intelligence
   - Meditation space for daily use
   - Meditation courses
   - Believes meditation improves employee mental health/well-being and the company's bottom line

4. Apple:
   - Gives employees thirty minutes each day to meditate at work
   - Meditation classes
   - Yoga on-site
   - Meditation room

5. Aetna:
   - Developed and offer two mindfulness programs: 1) Viniyoga Stress Reduction and Mindfulness at Work — in collaboration with Duke University 2) eMindful and the American Viniyoga Institute. Both programs showed participants enjoyed significant improvement in perceived stress level and heart rate measurements, improving their bodies' ability to manage stress
   - Meditation
   - Yoga classes

- One hour of yoga a week decreased stress levels in employees by a third, reducing healthcare costs by an average of $2,000 a year per employee

6. Intel:
    - Awake@Intel mindfulness program improves happiness, well-being, ideas, insights, creativity, quality of work relationships, ability to focus, mental clarity, and engagement

7. Green Mountain Coffee Roasters:
    - Monthly daylong mindfulness retreats to employees, family members, friends, and the community as a whole

8. Target:
    - Mindfulness meditation training

9. Deutsche Bank:
    - Meditation classes
    - Meditation room

10. HBO:
    - Free yoga classes
    - Meditation classes

11. Yahoo:
    - Meditation classes
    - Meditation rooms

12. Samsung:
    - Meditation training

13. AOL Time Warner:
    - Meditation classes during day
    - Meditation room

14. Nike:
    - Yoga
    - Meditation classes
    - Meditation room

15. Prentice Hall Publishing:
    - "Quiet Room" for meditation

16. Proctor and Gamble:
    - Meditation courses
    - Meditation spaces

17. Lululemon:
    - Yoga classes

18. Mobify:
    - Twice a week yoga classes

19. Dow Chemicals:
    - "Practicing Mindfulness for Positive Life Change"

20. BuildDirect:
    - Weekly yoga class

21. Ford Motor Company:
    - Mindfulness training

22. Salesforce:
    - Mindfulness training

23. Whole Foods:
    - Mindfulness training
    - Tibetan bowl meditation

So, do your research into these mind-body-spirit energy arts. Commit to practicing one or more of them for at least six months as their benefits are experiential and accumulative. If you notice that you're gaining benefits from your practice, consider introducing them into your culture and encouraging your people to practice them. You'll need to be brave, have a quiet rebel mindset, and be a true leader.

I'd like to acknowledge and give credit for some of the above information. It was gathered from the following two online sources: OnlineMBA[16] and *Harvard Business Review*.[17]

PART SIX:
BRINGING IT ALL TOGETHER –
COMPLETING THE CIRCLE

The Way of Effortless Leadership
Chapter 27 – Summary

It All Starts and Ends with You!

In summary, the Way of Effortless Leadership shows you that you're a microcosm of your organization and the natural world. For quick reference, use "model" in Chapter 9. You need to allow nature to inform your perception, thoughts, feelings, way of being, and actions to be truly effective. It's paradoxical and asks that you slow down, still your mind, expand your awareness, do and intervene less, use simplicity, and work smarter to be efficient and effective. It recognizes that growth and health are one and the same and can't be disentangled. It reconnects you to nature and your own human nature and helps you enter an effortless and productive state of flow. It requires that you be a conscious leader and tend to your own personal mind-body-spirit cultivation first. It's the way of health and sustainable growth for you, your people, your organization, and the planet. It enables you to create change and transformation in the same way nature does without producing resistance or opposition. It's about relaxing into a natural state where you and others can experience the freedom to be and self-express.

We've seen that the universe evolves from simple to complex, is energy-based, and creates by changing frequencies or vibrations and following natural growth cycles that transform energy. See the big-picture, forego goals that separate, and choose ones that unite people and the planet, that serve the greater good and personal, team, organizational, and societal evolution. Cultivate love, humility, patience, playfulness, and stillness within yourself. Act from your authentic vision and values, cultivating a culture of compassion and trust. Asking your people to join you in cocreating a better world will bring out their natural drive to help you realize it.

The Way is natural, simple, joyful, and awe-inspiring because it simply requires that you open your awareness; listen to nature (Wu Chi), your true nature (Zi Ran), and your surroundings; and then create a harmonious climate where others can do the same. **Wu Wei, effortless effort, is nature's way.** To follow her, **you must let go and forego the use of force and control. Instead**, be awake and aware, think holistically, use simplicity, relaxed intention, and do the absolute minimum to achieve your goal.

Wu Wei, effortless or forceless action, is the key principle. It's counterintuitive but works. When you push your people, you create an equal and opposite reaction or force by making them want to actively or passively resist. See yourself as the tai chi master who has cultivated his whole mind-body-spirit and developed awareness and sensitivity to everything around him and uses his relaxed, coordinated body and intention to move the "opponent" with a light touch by taking them in the direction they're leaning.

Continue to ask yourself: "Do I take time to meditate and return to the Tao? Am I leading from my heart? Are my values and vision clear and will I uphold them even if it means personal sacrifice, less financial gain, or short-term corporate success? Is my primary aim to create a living microcosm in my organization of the world in which I want to live? Am I creating a safe, peaceful climate? Am I creating a culture that really frees up, inspires, and encourages individual evolution so that people become self-so?"

Following nature's way will not only make you a better leader but will also make you happier. The old saying "the good things in life are free" is largely true. Stuff, prestige, fame, and fortune won't make you happy. Recent studies have shown that money only makes a real difference to your happiness up to an income of $75,000 a year. The more stuff you have, the more attention you pay to it and, ironically, the more it controls you and limits your peace of mind.

Matt Killingsworth created an iPhone app, TrackYourHappiness.org for his doctoral research at Harvard University. It allowed him to gather 650,000 real-time reports from over 15,000 people from all ages, walks of life, income, and education ranges from over eighty countries. One key learning from his study is that people are much happier when they're **present focused** than when they're "mind wandering" even if they're doing something they dislike. This highlights the importance of mindfulness and meditation. Putting everything aside and just being with your people, helping them succeed, will make you happier and will have a similar effect on them.

Remember, a relaxed body creates a calm mind. A calm mind creates a relaxed body and both work to lift the spirit. Leading from your heart and showing kindness, compassion, and love is important. That's the mind-body-spirit connection. You need to balance all three

The Way of Effortless Leadership

to be a truly effective leader. Following the Way, you enable yourself to develop what tai chi calls "internal power." You will learn to intentionally develop and direct your qi for the greater health and greater good.

The Way of Leadership is simple and requires relaxation, simplicity, awareness, compassion, and letting go. It works with human nature. It will provide your people with the climate they need to succeed. However, it may not always be easy because it all begins and ends with your own self-awareness and ability to change. Seeing yourself clearly and changing your habits takes time as you grapple with your own ego, resistance to change and impatience. In addition, your "monkey mind" will want to entice you with the latest fad and pull you off-course. Don't listen to it. Thank your thoughts and recommit to mastering the Way.

Take the pressure off yourself. Stop striving for perfection in yourself. Show your vulnerability. Your people want your attention, stillness, sincerity, self-awareness, caring, patience, playfulness, and positive intention. Show them those qualities and watch them thrive. However, you have to be sincere and consistent for it to work. If you try to fake it to coerce them or to enhance your image or position, people will sense it, and it will backfire.

Relax your expectations of others. Expecting perfection makes people fearful and play it safe. People who are fearful of trying new things rarely create or innovate. Encourage a culture where exploration and failure are encouraged as part of learning, growing, and creating.

Adopt a mastery mindset and keep flowing with nature's way. See the Way as a practice, not a quick fix. Commit to practicing the Way for the long haul. Your people will notice and appreciate your newfound relaxed awareness, openness, compassion, and trust. Yes, you'll hit learning plateaus and dips, but over time, you'll gain more skills and self-mastery. You'll wow your people and produce results that will amaze you.

Remember:

- Meditate to connect to the Tao (nature's way) in stillness (Wu Chi). This will inform how you need to BE, what you need to DO and enable you to HAVE the results.

- **Always use Wu Wei (effortless effort or forceless action) in everything you do.** Think strategically as to what changes will produce the most leverage to reach your collective vision and give it the lightest touch. Be minimalistic. Introduce and do the absolute minimum to achieve your goals. When in doubt, do less. If you notice yourself forcing something or controlling someone, stop it, sit back, relax, open your awareness, listen, and let nature take its course.

- Do no harm. Protect the dignity of others at all times. Appreciate the sacred "Atman"/BEING behind the worker. Do not intentionally ignore, harm, insult, humiliate, or in any way disregard or disrespect anyone. Challenge ideas but protect your relationship with each person.

- Continually improve your vibrations and cultivate your character, and your people will gladly follow you.

- Seek to achieve a state of Kong where you're relaxed and free of rigid beliefs about yourself and others.

- Soft overcomes hard. Lead from your heart chakra. Be compassionate, loving, sincere, caring, and empathetic. Use sensitivity and listening skills to understand and feel people's experience.

- Nature is seasonal. It balances stillness and rest with movement, activity and growth. Follow its lead. Always create opportunities for both you and your people to have an equal balance of both.

- Stay aware of what you're experiencing from moment to moment, without allowing yourself to get hooked. Notice your opinions, expectations, likes, and dislikes without creating a rigid story around them.

- Use your clear intention and imagination (yi mind) to visualize successful outcomes, but then detach from them.

The Way of Effortless Leadership

- Be patient, still, and compassionate.

- Coach others to cultivate their stillness, character, humility, compassion, and patience. Their growth will inspire and reenergize you.

- Create a culture that's open, flexible, moving, trusting, collaborative, and communicative; provide opportunity for rest, relaxation, distraction, and fun.

- Realize that everything and everyone resists being forced to change and being told what to do, so play gentle push hands. Don't over- or under-extend yourself. Be sensitive to the feelings and impressions you're receiving. Think about making progress by stepping forward a few paces and having to step back every once in a while. Partner with people during change, lead from behind.

- When something or someone comes at you forcefully, smile and relax into your body, stay aware, be dynamically balanced (Zhong Din), and thank them (in your mind) for helping you master yourself. Hold a positive impression of them while you engage in managing conflict. See and separate the valuable BEING behind the intransigent position.

- Be curious and nonjudgmental.

- Encourage each person to be Zi-ran, differentiated, meaning to be fully self-expressive (self-so) yet connected to you and the team.

- Forgive. This creates good qi.

- Take up mind-body self-cultivation exercises like tai chi, yoga, and qigong, and encourage others to do so.

- Start meetings with a short meditation, followed by each person sharing something for which they're grateful.

- Breathe naturally, be mindful, and get outside into nature often.

Surrender, let go of control, and gain it.

"At the heart of each of us, whatever our imperfections, there exists a silent pulse of perfect rhythm, made up of wave forms and resonances, which is absolutely individual and unique, and yet which connects us to everything in the universe." —George Leonard, *The Silent Pulse*

"The power of the people, so much stronger than the people in power." —Bono (Vancouver Joshua Tree Tour – May 2017)

"When the power of love overcomes the love of power, the world will know peace." —Jimi Hendrix

NOTE TO THE READER

Thank you for purchasing and reading my book. I hope you enjoyed it and that you can use it in your life and work. I'd appreciate it if you'd take a moment to review this book on Amazon and Goodreads. Your feedback is important to me and will help me grow as a writer and understand your needs.

You can reach me on Goodreads and at my website kgjohnston.com.

Keep in touch by signing up for my newsletter to receive future updates on contests, new books, launches, giveaways, signed copies, events, special pricing, freebies, reader surveys, photos, and insight into what's influencing me, my writing process, and new adventures.

GLOSSARY OF TERMS AND CONCEPTS

Chinese: Tai Chi/Taoist/Buddhist Concepts

De – Proper adherence to the Tao.

Dong Jing – Understand and direct or control the chi energy.

Kong – A relaxed state of mind that is empty and free of rigid beliefs about oneself and others.

Hui-lin-Din-Jin – "Erect head, empty neck." This is proper posture and allows the qi energy to flow naturally.

Jing – Sexual energy, original biological energy or essence.

Lu – Diverting an opponent's force into emptiness or nothingness, thereby neutralizing it.

Meridians – Part of Chinese medicine. Meridians are invisible energy pathways that circulate qi/chi through our body.

Qi/Chi – A Chinese word meaning aliveness, the flow of life force energy, or life breath. It is also known in different parts of the world as ki or prana. It can be likened to the science fiction "force" in *Star Wars*.

Shen – Spirit.

Sung – Relaxation and tranquility.

Tai Chi – The Supreme Ultimate. Tai Chi is The Tao in activity, expressed through the interplay of yin and yang.

The Tao – The way or the how of nature.

Tin Jin – Listening strength. Allows one to find out the intention and quality of the push hand's partner's force or position.

Tzu Jan – The state something or someone will be in if they are allowed to develop as their nature intended. The state of naturalness that is spontaneous.

Wu – Non-Being, limitlessness.

Wu Chi – Reality in a primordial state of nothingness or emptiness that within it contains limitless potential within it. "The Void."

Wu Wei – Effortless effort or effortless action.

Yi - The rational, intuitive, intentional mind.

Yin-Yang – Reality in a moving state of duality, of complementary

The Way of Effortless Leadership

"opposite" forces (positively and negatively charged) that was first described in the *I Ching* and, the *Tao Te Ching* and is an integral part of Chinese science, philosophy, arts, spirituality, martial arts and medicine. Yin and yang are two sides to an inseparable oneness or wholeness. Neither one is better nor worse, morally superior nor inferior to the other, as both are essential to each other.

Yu - Being.

Zhong Din "Centered Stability." Not passive stability but active stability. Maintaining one's equilibrium/ balance during change.

Zi Ran – Self-so. Everyone and everything follows its own nature.

Hindu/Yogic Concepts

Atman – Our real nature. We are all born divine, whole, and complete.

Chakras – Energy wheels or vortexes in our body. There are seven primary ones. The idea is to balance the energy in these vortexes. Too much or too little leads to imbalance and ill health.

Nadis – Are the same concept as Chinese meridians. They're invisible pathways that circulate prana through the body.

FURTHER READING

Alfie Kohn, *No Contest,* Houghton Mifflin Company, 1986.

Betsey Rippentrop and Eve Adamson, *The Complete Idiots Guide to Chakras*, Alpha (Penguin Group), 2009.

Bill Catlette, B and Richard Hadden R, *Contented Cows Give Better Milk: The Plain Truth About Employee Relations and Your Bottom Line,* Saltillo Press, 2000.

Christina Brown, *The Book of Yoga,* Paragon Publishing, 2002.

Dave Logan, John King, & Halee Fischer-Wright, *Tribal Leadership*, 2008.

David Gelles, *Mindful Work*, Houghton Mifflin Harcourt Publishing Company, 2015. How mindfulness works for companies.

David Rock, *Quiet Leadership*, HarperCollins Publishers, 2006.

David Rock, *Your Brain at Work*, HarperCollins Publishers, 2009.

Dr. Wen Zee, *Wu Style Tai Chi Chuan, Ancient Way to Health,* Blue Snake Books, 2002.

Dr. Yang Jwing-Ming, *Qigong Meditation-* Small Circulation, YMAA Publication Center, 2006.

Gary Anaka, *Your Magical Brain – How It Learns Best*, Portal Press, 2005.

Gervase Bush, *Clear Leadership,* Davies-Black Publishing, 2001.

Herbert Benson, with Miriam Z. Klipper M.D, *The Relaxation Response,* Harper Collins, 1975.

John Heider, *The Tao of Leadership*, Humanics Limited, 1985.

John Wright, "**The High Cost of Employee Disengagement.**" **tinyurl.com/WrightDisART**

Kenneth S. Cohen, *The Way of Qigoing – The Art and Science of Chinese Energy Healing,* The Random House Publishing Group, 1997.

Lee Bolman. L & and Terrence Deal T., *Reframing Organizations: Artistry, Choice and Leadership*, John Wiley & Sons, Inc., 2008.

Margaret Wheatley, *Leadership and the New Science: Discovering Order in a Chaotic World.* Berrett-Koehler Publishers, 2006.

Marshall J. Cook and Laura Poole, *Effective Coaching* – Second Edition, McGraw Hill, 2011.

Marvin Weisbord,, M., *Productive Workplaces: Dignity, Meaning and Community in the 21st Century,* Josey Bass, 2012.

Paul Hellyer, *The Money Mafia: A World in Crisis,* Trine Day, 2014.

Percy Willard, *The Sustainability Advantage,* New Society Publishers, 2002.

Peter M. Senge, C. Otto Scharmer, Joseph Jaworski, and Betty Sue Flowers, *Presence: Human Purpose and the Field of the Future,* Crown Business, 2008.

Peter Senge, Bryan Smith, Nina Kruschwitz, Joe Laur, and Sara Schley, *The Necessary Revolution – How Organizations Are Working Together to Create a Sustainable World,* Broadway Books, 2010.

Peter Senge, *The Fifth Discipline – The Art & Practice of the Learning Organization,* Doubleday, 2006.

Sean Carroll, *The Particle at the End of the Universe*, Dutton, 2012.

Shari Jaeger Goodwin, *Take The Reins! 7 Secrets to Inspiring Leadership*, 2013.

Sharon Begley, *Train Your Mind, Change Your Brain*, Ballentine Books, 2008.

Stephen Cope, *Yoga and the Quest for the True Self,* Bantam Books, 1999.

Thich Nhat Hanh, *Anger,* The Berkley Publishing Group, 2001.

Wu Kung Cho, *Wu Style Tai Chi Chuan,* Jonathan Krehm on Behalf of the International Wu Style Tai Chi Chuan Federation. 2006.

www.wustyle.com (International Wu Style Tai Chi Chuan website)

Articles on Corporate Personhood

Corporate Personhood.
https://en.wikipedia.org/wiki/Corporate_personhood

When Did Companies Become People? Excavating The Legal Evolution
http://www.npr.org/2014/07/28/335288388/when-did-companies-become-people-excavating-the-legal-evolution

Treating Corporations as People
https://www.nytimes.com/2015/05/27/business/dealbook/treating-corporations-as-people.html

If Corporations Are People, They Should Act Like It
https://www.theatlantic.com/politics/archive/2015/02/if-corporations-are-people-they-should-act-like-it/385034/

Articles that Relate to Big Business and Mindfulness

Amazing Meditation 101 – The Way Google Does It!
tinyurl.com/AMED101

The Relationship Between Meditation and Productivity
tinyurl.com/MedProdART

CEO of AOL does Tai Chi for business & for life
tinyurl.com/CEOTaiChiART

Why Companies Are Turning To Meditation And Yoga To Boost The Bottom Line
tinyurl.com/CoMedYogART

Taiji Principles for Business and Life
tinyurl.com/TaijiBusLifeART

Compassion Articles:

Why Compassion in Business Makes Sense
tinyurl.com/CompBusART

Stanford Research: Compassion Aids Well-Being

tinyurl.com/CompWellART

The Compassionate Mind
tinyurl.com/COMPMIND

Top 10 Scientific Benefits of Compassion (Infographic)
tinyurl.com/Comp10BeneART

The Center for Compassion and Altruism Research and Education
ccare.stanford.edu/research/

Articles on Business Leadership

Why (Some) Psychopaths Make Great CEOs
tinyurl.com/CEOpsychoART

7 Habits of Natural Leaders
tinyurl.com/7HabNatLeadART

END NOTES

1. Janine Benyus's TED talk on Biomimicry
tinyurl.com/BenyusTED

2. Carl Safina's TED talk on What Animals Are Thinking and Feeling.
tinyurl.com/SafinaTED

3. China looks at plans to ban petrol and diesel cars.
http://tinyurl.com/Chinaecars

4. John Hagelin's video on YouTube to learn how the universe uses vibration to create matter. tinyurl.com/HagelinVID

5. Parallel Universes and How to Change Reality.
tinyurl.com/ParallelVID

6. Dr Quantum - Double Slit Experiment. tinyurl.com/Dr-QVID

7. Michio Kaku's videos. The Universe in a Nutshell and String Theory
tinyurl.com/KakuNutVID   tinyurl.com/KakuStringVID

8. Dr. Bruce Lipton on Epigenetics: The Science of Human Empowerment. tinyurl.com/LiptonVID

9. Except from Oprah Winfrey talks TM with Dr. Mehmet Oz -TM Blog,
by Mario Orsatti on 12/08/2011. http://tinyurl.com/OpraTM

10. National Geographic "This Is Your Brain on Nature."
tinyurl.com/NGMbrainART

11. David Suzuki "Nature Calms the Brain and Heals the Body"
tinyurl.com/SuzukiBrainART

12. University of Minnesota. How Does Nature Impact Our Wellbeing? tinyurl.com/UMNnatureART

13. International Coaching Federation. Core Competencies.
tinyurl.com/ICFcompART

14. Stuart Brown's TED talk on "Play is More Than Fun."
tinyurl.com/BrownTED

15. Push Hands videos:

    Wu Style Push Hands – Ma Jiang Bao
    tinyurl.com/PHWuBao –

Wu Style Push Hands – Eddie Wu.
tinyurl.com/PHWuWu -

Wu Style Push Hands – Shen Tiegen.
tinyurl.com/PHWuTiegen –

Chen Style Push Hands.
tinyurl.com/PHChen -

Wu Style 108 Fast Form – Eddie Wu
tinyurl.com/PHWuWuFast –

Wu Style 108 Traditional Square Standard Form – Eddie Wu.
tinyurl.com/PHWuWuTrad –

16. OnlineMBA. 10 Big Companies That Promote Employee Meditation. **tinyurl.com/OMBA10CoART**

17. Kimberly Schaufenbuel. Why Google, Target, and General Mills Are Investing in Mindfulness. *Harvard Business Review.* **tinyurl.com/HBRmoreCosART**

Printed in Poland
by Amazon Fulfillment
Poland Sp. z o.o., Wrocław